The Principal's Guide to Instructional Improvement:

Theory to Practice

Robert Krajewski

Foreword by Gordon Cawelti

ROWMAN & LITTLEFIELD EDUCATION

A division of
ROWMAN & LITTLEFIELD PUBLISHERS, INC.
Lanham • Boulder • New York • Toronto • Plymouth, UK

Published by Rowman & Littlefield Education
A division of Rowman & Littlefield Publishers, Inc.
A wholly owned subsidary of The Rowman & Littlefield Publishing Group, Inc.
4501 Forbes Boulevard, Suite 200, Lanham, Maryland 20706
http://www.rowmaneducation.com

10 Thornbury Road, Plymouth PL6 7PP, United Kingdom

British Library Cataloguing in Publication Information Available

Library of Congress Cataloging-in-Publication Data

Krajewski, Robert J.
  The principal's guide to instruction improvement : theory to practice / Robert Krajewski.
    p. cm.
  Includes bibliographical references and index.
  ISBN 978-1-61048-640-8 (cloth : alk. paper) — ISBN 978-1-61048-641-5 (pbk. : alk. paper) — ISBN 978-1-61048-642-2 (electronic)
  1. Teachers—In-service training. 2. Teacher-principal relationships. 3. School improvement programs. I. Title.
  LB1731.K69 2012
  370.71'1—dc23

                                                                        2012000238

∞™ The paper used in this publication meets the minimum requirements of American National Standard for Information Sciences—Permanence of Paper for Printed Library Materials, ANSI/NISO Z39.48-1992.

Printed in the United States of America

Contents

Foreword

Our nation's schools have been heavily criticized over the past several years with a plethora of suggestions for how they can and should be "reformed." Many of these proposals are made by people who know very little about teaching and learning, while some suggestions are thoughtful and merit careful consideration. The "reforms" proposed by politicians are often characterized by concern for increasing *competition* among schools, as is the case with charter schools, or by increasing the *incentives* for teachers as with merit pay plans.

The fact is that research summarizing the effects of such plans for increasing competition and incentives among schools and teachers has tended to not show any improved student achievement when compared with more traditional plans. This is not to say there have been no charter schools or merit pay plans that did not yield improved results, but rather that the *overall* effects of either approach have not demonstrated the kind of results advocates claim.

The repeated failure of these approaches to school improvement involving competition and incentives can be explained. I have never seen a teacher who was withholding services. Instead I am much more inclined to believe he or she has just never been taught or shown how to "teach better." And while paying car salesmen commissions based on sales probably does encourage them to sell more cars, that process and its variables are infinitely less complex than helping teachers provide learning experiences that can help all the students in a school to make substantial gains on important learning outcomes.

Fortunately we do know something about how such gains for all students can be accomplished. And this book makes an important contribution toward helping principals and others in a supervisory relationship with teachers acquire the skills *required* to actually *help* teachers expand the repertoire of skills needed in today's classroom. Clinical supervision skills have been refined over the past several decades to where a process is now described that respects teachers and enables supervisors to assist them in learning where and how they can improve their teaching and how to incorporate more effective techniques and teaching strategies into their daily routines. If a *trusting* relationship between supervisors and teachers is to be maintained, then clinical supervision must remain separated from the anxieties often present in required teacher and principal "evaluation" systems. This book focuses on "growth," not evaluation.

My own experience tells me that extensive use of the clinical supervision process and interaction analysis, along with regular use of team planning and technology, will invariably result in improved student achievement. Helping principals and supervisors acquire clinical supervision and interaction analysis skills is a key element to actually accomplishing substantially improved student achievement rather than placing hope in the effects that are often believed to result from focusing on school competition plans or increasing incentives for teachers.

Gordon Cawelti, August 2011
Editor, *Handbook of Research on Improving Student Achievement* (2004)
Senior Scholar, *High Student Achievement: How Six School Districts Changed into High-Performance Systems* (2001)

Acknowledgments

While an acknowledgments page is not always found in a text, I believe it is essential in this case. The difficulty in writing this page is whom to include, and why. So the acknowledgments are threefold—content, inspiration, and preparation of the manuscript.

Content. From the beginning of my higher-education career I have always been interested in the principal's role in instructional leadership, the main ingredient of which is clinical supervision. The first acknowledgment thus is afforded to someone I've never met—Bob Goldhammer, whose pursuit of humaneness and rapport in clinical supervision is legendary. Next is my former colleague Bob Anderson, who carried on Bob's passion. He and I were a good team because we respected each other's beliefs and melded them into two revisions of Goldhammer's text, as well as a lifelong friendship. Next, in no respective order, are Dwight Allen, who helped me with microteaching; Ned Flanders, who helped me with FIAS; and many principals with whom I have worked and from whom I have learned.

Inspiration. In one of my initial writing attempts, an editor rejected my first submission of a principal/supervision article and sent me a one-and-one-half-page reason why. Devastated, I put the article away for several months, then read it again and discovered he was right. I revised according to his suggestions, and "I Never Met a Teacher I Didn't Like" was printed and became my inspiration. Again, in no respective order, Bob Anderson, Gordon Cawelti, Fred Wilhelms, and other distinguished educators—mainly principals—from whom I continue to learn have inspired me as well. My wife also afforded inspiration and ideas. Each of us, though, has to have a favorite, and mine is our son Ryean, whose courage I could not begin to match.

Manuscript Preparation. Two education students, Beth Niebuhr, an undergraduate, and Xee Chang, a graduate student, have not only helped with typing, but also kept me on task. Their help was great.

Introduction

Entering my first year of teaching at a large semisuburban integrated high school, an assistant principal called me in to talk. "Bob," he said, "I'm glad you are with us as a math teacher. It is important that you teach well, but even more important is who you are. Students will learn more by watching what you do as a person." Several years later, Fred Wilhelm's coined statement that "what a teacher/supervisor is is more important than anything he does" reaffirmed that initial advice.

It is a double pleasure to have worked with and learned from many instructional improvement scholar and practitioner colleagues who are exemplars of those words. This book wouldn't have been possible without knowledge and "moxie" gained from professional and personal experiences with them.

Too often we hear the word *evaluation* when people talk about teachers and principals. As recently as last week, for example, *Education Week* featured an article about our principals' organizations working together to develop yet another principal evaluation process.

This user-friendly book will neither focus on evaluation nor mention it. Rather, it focuses on providing principals both foundation and specific skills to enhance teacher and principal professional growth in improving instruction and student achievement. Featured are elements of rapport not available in any other text; clinical supervision as seen through a newer, more flexible process; and explanation of objective interaction analysis instruments that are practical and easy to use.

A special feature is a very detailed self-teaching presentation of Flanders Interaction Analysis System, a valuable tool for growth. Most important is the human element featured in the explanations, fueled by the notion that the person using the tool(s) is more important than the tool(s).

Former colleague and coauthor Bob Anderson thought that training in clinical supervision (to a great extent) ought to be in schools where real kids are taught by real professionals. The payoff, he thought—and I concur—is when principals trained in clinical supervision are in the classroom using those skills to help teachers improve.

Lastly, I am pleased that Gordon Cawelti, another champion of instructional improvement, wrote an eloquent foreword to this book. He too has long led the quest to provide better instruction for students.

Bob Krajewski

Section I

INTRODUCTION

As the title suggests, *The Principal's Guide to Instructional Improvement: Theory to Practice* is divided into two sections, theory and practice. By structuring the book in two separate pieces, there is equal focus on both the foundation of supervision and its implementation, allowing for complete understanding and application in schools.

This first section primarily discusses the theory and foundation of supervision. Tracing the evolution of school supervision from basic school inspection by ministers, selectmen, and committees, to evaluation by the first superintendents, and then finally to instructional improvement by school principals, chapter 1 begins with a brief history of school supervision in the United States. This chapter concludes with a focus on clinical supervision, discussing both its origination at Harvard during the 1950s and its present-day use in contemporary schooling.

Lastly, this section features a never-before-explained foundation of rapport, the constant element in the author's clinical supervision model. Rapport is composed of content and process, both of which are explained and discussed. By thoroughly reviewing the rapport foundation, school principals will have a better understanding of the model, which they can then explain to their teachers.

After reading this first section, you will feel confident enough to implement the process/practice material provided in the second section. When you do, it is a new ball game; both teacher and principal will grow tremendously. Guaranteed.

Chapter One

Abridged History of Supervision and Clinical Supervision

Understandably, America's earliest schools were usually imports from England and reflected long-standing European school models. Religion played an important role in New England colonial schools in both curriculum and conduct. Thus religious instruction, comprised of learning to read the Bible, was prominent. The church set the curriculum, prescribed teaching methods, and maintained discipline.

Schooling often began in the home with and by the family. As population increased, some homes became schools taught by a respected woman (then called a dame). That was the beginning of dame schools. Further growth spawned local schools—for those who could afford to attend. Curriculum broadened. Teaching of reading and writing was generally accepted. Religious instruction, however, required attention by proper authorities, and ministers were deemed the best-qualified community members to judge teachers' efforts.

Prominent laymen whose children attended local schools soon became interested in the school and teaching problems and began introducing those problems at town or district meetings. In an attempt to address their concerns, towns and districts chose committees to study school problems and make recommendations but gave the committees no authority. That wasn't efficient.

As school problems became more complex, a "selectman" was chosen to accompany ministers in school visits. Eventually clergy control lessened. By 1709, professional administration and supervision began to take root via these selectmen who made school "inspections."

The first attempts at supervising schools thus had a tri-focus:

- assuming autocratic rule
- inspecting and removing weak teachers
- ensuring that teachers conform to laymen committee standards.

From the beginning, supervision by selectmen had a negative effect on teachers. Teachers became frustrated. Ministers talked about them, and so did many town and district leaders at public meetings. Small wonder, then, that "supervision" became an immediate negative. Teachers equated supervision with "inspection." The negative feeling exists among many teachers yet today.

These selectmen inspected the schools' physical conditions and teachers' tasks—including that of custodian. Among the selectmen was one layman who had more interest or aptitude for school visitation. Eventually the selectman role evolved into a position known as school visitor or school inspector, a layman who served without pay. Laymen visits were frequent and announced. Supervision by laypeople lingered for more than a hundred years.

When school visit responsibilities became increasingly heavy, it was difficult to find competent layman visitors who could take the time from their own occupation to make the required visits and reports. Out of sheer necessity, then, school visitors were given token payments for their services. It was at this point that supervision took its first professional step away from religious and lay inspections of colonial days.

As area populations continued to grow, so did school attendance. Cities grew larger, school systems and districts became larger, and the number of schools to be visited increased. Still, the position of supervisor was not declared. Instead, in addition to or replacement for the school visitor/inspector, people were selected as a manager or treasurer, and as part of their duties, they were expected to visit and inspect schools and teachers. In the mid-1800s, the manager/treasurer role was converted to superintendent, a professional person who was really more of an office clerk, with some technical supervisory duties and occasional school-visitor responsibilities.

Professionally, then, most educational historians agree that supervision in American schools developed from, and was an integral part of, the school superintendency. As noted herein, superintendents' supervision influence was the role played by school districts' laypersons who were called upon to fulfill the "inspection" function. Supervision as inspection, according to modern supervision writers, lost its impact in the latter part of the 1800s or the beginning of the 1900s. Although still in partial use today, inspection as the primary supervision tool has lost much appeal.

At the beginning of the 1900s, prompted by school expansion and inadequate teacher preparation, superintendents began to perform more teacher supervision tasks. Why? The *First Yearbook of Superintendence* reported a 1911 study that found both elementary and secondary teachers had only three or four years of training beyond elementary school. It was no surprise, then, that in the 1920s, even in large cities, superintendents ranked supervision as their highest performing activity, followed by determining subject content in curricula. But this was a catch-22, as superintendents were not trained to work with improving specific teaching strategies.

As superintendents' duties increased, it was obvious that they needed help in their supervisory role. Principals seemed to be the natural choice to assist them. The founding of the National Association of Secondary School Principals (1916) and National Association of Elementary School Principals (1920) was instrumental. Both organizations stressed that principals lead their schools in instructional improvement. By the late 1920s, school principals were expected to share supervisory responsibilities with the school superintendent. Just as with superintendents, however, principals were in a catch-22, as they were not trained to work with improving specific teaching strategies either.

Further, most principals also had teaching responsibilities. Their titles included head teacher, headmaster, or principal teacher. Some principals even taught full time. Their history parallels the superintendents' regarding supervision of teachers for instructional improvement.

Instructional leadership requires proficiency in both instruction and curriculum. Founded in 1857, the National Education Association (NEA) established various committees to help teachers grow. In 1929, NEA's Department of Supervisors and Directors of Instruction (DSDI) and Society for Curriculum Study (SCS) were established to professionally recognize both supervisors' and principals' significant role in the improvement of learning. DSDI and SCS soon had overlapping goals and membership. And they should have, as supervision requires both interpersonal communication skills and some knowledge of varied curriculum.

To better serve instructional leadership, DSDI and SCS merged in 1943 to form the Association for Supervision and Curriculum Development (ASCD). No longer an affiliate of NEA, ASCD has more than 160,000 teacher, supervisor, and administrator members who are interested in teacher and administrator professional development. Despite these advances, however, classroom supervision continues to take an inspectoral or evaluation approach.

When Sputnik was launched in 1957, our nation went into a frenzy that caused supervisors to concentrate on curriculum development, specifically science, mathematics, and foreign languages—aided by federal dollars. Clinical supervision's emergence in the late 1950s at Harvard University caused a major shift in supervision, as supervisors became more involved in classroom instruction, curriculum, and rapport.

Recently, coaching and group dynamics became key functions of supervision. Today, however, the "inspection" function of supervision lingers. When

WHEN	WHAT	WHO
1600-1850	Inspection & Evaluation	Selectmen
1850-1920	Scientific Management	Superintendent/Supervisor
1920-1945	Democratic Interaction Approach	Supervisor
1945-1965	Supervision w/ Curriculum Development	Curriculum Supervisor
1965-	Impact of Clinical Supervision Ideas	Curriculum/Instructional Supervisor
1970-1985	Group Dynamics/Peer Emphasis	Curriculum/Instructional Supervisor
1990-2008	Coaching/Instructional Supervision	Instructional Supervisor
2005-	Instructional Supervision	Increasing emphasis for Principals

Figure 1.1

supervision is attempted, evaluation frequently becomes the focus. We have not been able to erase that roadblock to teacher development for improving instruction.

Figure 1.1 summarizes essential characteristics of supervision, broadly defined, during eight periods of educational history.

A. SUPERVISION

As noted above, instructional supervision is central to effective teaching. In its earliest form, however, supervision was inspection, mainly of facilities; in addition to teaching, the teachers' role included maintenance of the school facility. Many years passed before supervision's focus moved toward inspection of teaching. Supervision development paralleled administration development:

- as supervision became more collegial, so did administration;
- as supervision began to incorporate leadership, so did administration; and
- as supervision included more group dynamics, so did administration.

In education, the term *supervision* refers to both person and process. In his powerful 1973 ASCD booklet, *Supervision in a New Key,* 1968–1972 ASCD secretary/director Fred Wilhelms said that supervision is the "nervous system" of the school that enables adaptation and change. Without adaptation and change there will be little to no instructional improvement.

Although supervision is the dimension of the teaching profession concerned with making instruction more effective, supervision definitions sometimes lack in specificity.

1. "All activities by which educational officers may express leadership in the improvement of teaching" (DSDI, 1931, p. 3).
2. "All efforts of designated school officials directed toward providing leadership to teachers and other educational workers in the improvement of instruction" (Good, 1945, p. 539).
3. "That phase of school administration which focuses primarily upon the achievement of the appropriate instructional expectations of educational systems" (Eye, Netzer, & Krey, 1971, p. 30).
4. "Those activities that improve the quality of teaching and stimulate professional growth and the attainment of 'stretch goals' of all participants, thereby nurturing a healthy, invigorating and effective work culture" (Goldhammer, Anderson, & Krajewski, 1993, p. 31).

Historically, then, supervision has had a tough existence—from the very beginning of schools in America. Religion played the most important role in early education. Rapid population growth brought problems in teaching and administration. Solving the problems was not a consistent or enduring endeavor. Inspection was the major function of both supervision and administration. Unfortunately, as time went on, education experts and laypersons alike had much difficulty agreeing on a supervision definition and the supervisor role. Furthermore, supervision never was able to shed "inspection" and "evaluation" stigmas.

Today, lack of a specific definition of supervision is due to the wide range of people who perform supervisory tasks, the varied titles they have, and the variety of responsibilities they are assigned. Some supervisors are responsible for:

- the whole of curriculum, K-12
- a specific subject throughout the elementary school grades
- a specific subject in the secondary grades
- a specific subject, K-12
- all subjects for a grade or grades.

Some instructional supervisors:

- work in the district or central office and are expected to provide teachers with curriculum materials or schedule instructional improvement staff development for teachers. Some of these supervisors seldom see the inside of the classroom and may not have face-to-face contact with teachers.
- spend a majority of their working day observing teachers in classrooms.
- serve their instructional improvement duties accomplishing both district office responsibilities and classroom observation responsibilities.

Given this ambiguous situation, more and more principals are expected to supervise instruction. They are expected to observe teachers with a specific instructional improvement rubric. Yet, as superintendents before them, they are faced with a catch-22. Principals seldom are offered university preparation or staff development opportunities to learn how to objectively analyze instruction.

This text is designed to offer principals self-development and self-instruction skills for improving instruction using objective data in a humanistic way—*for teacher growth, not evaluation.*

B. CLINICAL SUPERVISION

In the latter 1970s, ASCD commissioned a national working group on "Role and Responsibilities of Supervisors." Our task was to review empirical research and literature to gather current information on the role of the instructional supervisor.

In our research we conducted telephone interviews with executive directors of American Association of Colleges for Teacher Education, American Association of School Administrators, American Federation of Teachers, Association for Supervision and Curriculum Development, Council of Professors of Instructional Supervision, National Association of Elementary School Principals, National Association of Secondary School Principals, National Education Association, Professors of Curriculum, and representative members from those groups— twenty-one persons total.

When we asked what courses should be included in instructional supervisor (and principal) preparation programs, forty-nine of the sixty-three suggestions they provided included a course that involved the techniques and practices of clinical supervision. Those surveyed noted that interaction among people involved in instructional improvement was central to learning success. Further, they said that clinical supervision is THE process in which instructional people receive the best insight into the quality of the teacher-student interaction.

Clinical supervision was developed by Morris Cogan and his Harvard colleagues in the 1950s. Cogan chaired the secondary education internship program and the secondary master of arts in teaching (MAT) program. The MAT program comprised mornings of summer student teaching in Newton, Massachusetts, schools supervised by a master teacher under the guidance of a Harvard professor. Master teachers were selected from throughout the country. Each master teacher was responsible for about five interns who individually would teach small groups of students or the whole class.

When one intern taught, the others observed, along with an observation team leader. Observer(s) scripted the lesson; that is, they tried to write in words all the interaction during the lesson (as we will explain later, this was rather inefficient because [a] it was too difficult to write everything, [b] the scripter could not follow the lesson interaction while writing, and [c] conference feedback was more subjective than objective). In the afternoon, the observation team provided feedback, via the scripting, to the intern who taught. Intern afternoon activities also included reflection, planning, and methods courses.

During fall semester, interns taught full time in a nearby school district. Their spring semester was spent in graduate study at Harvard. Completing those activities led to the MAT degree and teacher certification. MAT programs soon spread throughout the country, following the Harvard model or variations of it. The programs are still popular today.

Robert Anderson was Cogan's Harvard colleague. Anderson chaired Harvard's elementary education preparation and elementary MAT program. Elementary summer interns taught in the Lexington, Massachusetts, district. Team teaching was introduced in the elementary program in 1957, and soon thereafter in the secondary program.

So Newton and Lexington schools became the "clinics" in which "clinical supervision" was birthed and refined.

Cogan's model was a rigid eight-step "cycle" process, comprised of:

1. establishing the teacher-supervisor relationship
2. planning with the teacher
3. planning the observation strategy
4. observing the agreed-upon lesson
5. analyzing the lesson
6. planning the conference strategy
7. effecting the conference
8. renewing the planning.

Robert Goldhammer, Cogan's doctoral student at Harvard, refined the clinical supervision process to five "stages" while serving several years as an observation team leader in the Lexington program.

1. Preobservation conference
2. Observation
3. Analysis and strategy
4. Supervision conference
5. Postconference strategy

Both his model and dissertation emphasized the "human" element in clinical supervision.

Both Cogan and Goldhammer wrote a book on clinical supervision. Ironically, Goldhammer, the student, published his book first. His landmark text *Clinical Supervision: Special Methods for the Supervision of Teachers,* was published in 1969. After Goldhammer passed away in 1968, Bob Anderson edited and completed the text. Cogan published his text, *Clinical Supervision*, in 1973. Anderson and Krajewski published the second (1980) and third (1993) editions, respectively, of Goldhammer's text.

As a Duke doctoral student from 1968 to 1971, I self-taught clinical supervision, Flanders Interaction Analysis (FIAS), and microteaching—three objective ways of analyzing student-teacher interaction in the classroom. Via phone the Far West Regional Laboratory's Ned Flanders guided me in learning his system. Stanford's Dwight Allen and Bob Bush did likewise for my learning microteaching.

Duke's MAT was secondary, including summer methods and psychology courses to students with an undergraduate discipline-oriented degree. The students, as interns, then taught full day, full year, and took two graduate courses each semester at a university close to where they taught. The next summer they returned to Duke for more courses and graduated with a MAT degree.

In 1970–1971 Duke's MAT cohort comprised forty-one students who graduated from twenty-seven colleges and universities in fifteen states. I taught them microteaching, FIAS, and clinical supervision during their summer methods course. My dissertation analyzed effects of clinical supervision, videotaping, and FIAS matrix recordings on MAT interns. We used a true experimental design, with Minnesota Attitude Inventory, Graduate Record Exam, Stanford Teacher Appraisal Guide, and so on, as pretests for experimental and control groups.

During the academic year, I videotaped and performed FIAS and clinical supervision (via guided self-analysis) five times apiece with an experimental group of 20 middle and secondary MAT intern teachers in twenty schools in Virginia and North Carolina—a total of one hundred tapes. In contrast to the Harvard program, conference feedback for each lesson was using objective data from FIAS and video in a clinical supervision format. Duke faculty supervised the twenty-one-intern control group. We administered various post-tests as self-ratings, student ratings, supervisor ratings, Minnesota Teacher Attitude Inventory, and Stanford Teacher Competence Appraisal Guide to both groups and compared results.

I have continued to use these and other objective tools in supervising teachers from kindergarten through graduate school, and also college professors. At Texas Tech, we taught Individually Guided Education to Texas profes-

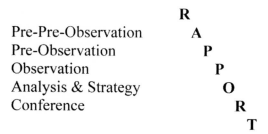

Figure 1.2

sors in a summer-long institute via the clinical supervision cycle. From these experiences I refined Goldhammer's model. The revision, shown in figure 1.2 and explained in chapter 3, has five steps that stress rapport and *rapport nurturance* throughout the entire process. Without the continual emphasis on rapport and rapport nurturance, any type of supervision, especially clinical supervision, will not be successful.

Clinical supervision is more clearly defined than supervision, as it offers an interactive process to improve instruction. Goldhammer et al. (1993) defined clinical supervision as:

> . . . supervision which draws upon data from first-hand observation of actual teaching . . . and involves face-to-face . . . interactions between observer(s) and person(s) observed in . . . analyzing the observed professional behaviors and seeks to . . . develop next steps toward improved performance. (p. 34)

According to Goldhammer et al. (1993), the clinical supervision concept has these characteristics. Clinical supervision:

1. is a deliberate intervention into the instructional process.
2. is a goal-oriented, objective, yet flexible, method to improve instruction.
3. assumes that the supervisor is competent in analyzing instruction.
4. assumes a professional working relationship between teacher(s) and supervisor(s).
5. requires a high degree of mutual trust, such as understanding, support, and commitment to growth.
6. is a technology (and uses technology) for improving instruction.

Principals should be exemplars of these characteristics and assure that teachers know and accept these characteristics. Though the principal has supervision responsibility, it is vital that both teachers and principal understand and accept their respective clinical supervision roles. Chapter 3 contains an explanation of these clinical supervision characteristics and their importance in the clinical supervision process.

SUMMARY

Imported from Europe, early American education was rooted in religion and selectivity. It began, simply, in homes taught by family, then progressed to one volunteer teacher still in a home, called dame schools. Its curriculum evolved from reading the Bible to today's comprehensiveness. Educational supervision began on a sour note—inspection, first by ministers, then select-men, then school visitors, then superintendents. Today's supervision how-ever, has not been able to shed some of the negativity associated with inspec-tion, as some supervisors still sort of inspect. Further, today's supervision suffers from being too aligned with evaluation. Over time, principals have been expected to become more involved with instructional supervision, but their university preparation programs and staff development seldom prepare them adequately for this role. Thus they are in a catch-22, with many expecta-tions and little foundation.

Begun at Harvard in the 1950s, primarily under the guidance of Morris Co-gan, who worked with secondary education and secondary MAT interns, and Robert Anderson, who worked with elementary education and elementary MAT interns, clinical supervision is more detailed, accurate, and data driven than supervision. That detailed and accurate analysis of instruction came from a specific step program for clinical supervision—first Cogan's clinical supervision model, then Goldhammer's model, then Krajewski's model. The data-driven aspect has been refined by use of objective analysis instruments rather than the scripting used at Harvard in clinical supervision's formative stages. Yet today, in spite of its promise, it has been less than a major force in education. Several reasons, albeit not necessarily accurate, have contributed to that situation. The major one, though, revolves around *evaluation empha-sis prevalent in schools.* Supervision and clinical supervision concentrate on teacher and principal *growth,* not *evaluation.*

FAQS

Who were the main students in early American education? Wealthier boys who were being trained for the clergy.
Who were the first teachers? Mothers (dames) who taught children in their homes.

Who were the first school inspectors? Ministers.

Do selectmen still exist? Yes, mainly in Massachusetts, but they are on boards to deal with town matters.

Could superintendents effectively supervise classes? As school districts became larger, leadership responsibilities increased. Time and training became important factors.

Why is rapport stressed in clinical supervision? Because without it, one can't be successful in improving instruction.

Who chose your dissertation focus? I did, although initially I was encouraged to sit in the library stacks and do a library-type dissertation. My dissertation committee finally agreed to let me do this project.

Why were you determined to do it? Bob Goldhammer's passion and Bob Anderson's devotion to improve teaching and student achievement convinced me. Capstone projects should ultimately be developed to help students. It did not take me long to assume that same passion that Goldhammer had and the devotion to improving teaching and student achievement that Anderson had. And forty-one years later I still have the skills I learned at Duke and practice them when I prepare teachers and work with preparing principals.

Chapter Two

Rapport

A. DEFINITION

Rapport is a harmonious relationship among people. Integral to successful supervision of teaching, rapport always remains the principal's responsibility. Most dictionaries refer to rapport with words and phrases like *harmony* and *willingness to cooperate*. In a recent graduate supervision class, students offered several rapport definitions. Rapport, they said, is:

- a relationship between persons that makes it possible for them to easily relate to each other;
- a feeling of acceptance, comfort, respect, and encouragement to be ourselves; or
- a meaningful and productive relationship between two or more people.

Supervision is a collaborative, two-way street nourished by rapport. Without rapport, supervision will not be successful. Establish rapport early and make it a constant throughout the supervisory process. When you do that, conditions become more conducive for rewarding learning, growth, and success for the teacher, the students, and yourself. Rapport cannot be established and then left to progress on its own. When you nurture it, everyone will know it is there and it will grow and mature. But how do you do it?

Numerous books have advocated the importance of rapport. Yet few authors, if any, have offered a delineation of, or foundation for, rapport. Rapport does have a foundation. The foundation consists of both content (what and why) and process (how). Understanding the content "whats and whys" is prerequisite to learning the process "hows."

Rapport content comprises:

- supervision
- curriculum/specific subject matter
- instructional theory
- learning theory and styles
- motivation theory.

Rapport process comprises

- positive self-concept
- acceptance of self and others
- *communication*
- evolving learning of subject content
- moxie.

An explanation of these follows—first the content.

B. RAPPORT CONTENT

i. Supervision

Supervision, a collaborative ongoing effort to enhance instruction, is a precise parallel to good teaching.

Effective teachers are the learner "model" in their classes. Likewise, effective principals are the learner "model" in the supervision process (see figure 2.1). That's a crucial mindset for principals, as they must:

- First and foremost, learn and understand the content—the what and whys of supervision.
- Second, be a continual exemplar of learning.

ii. Curriculum/Specific Subject Matter

In addition to specific subject matter, curriculum encompasses *ALL* learning experiences students have under the guidance or direction of the school that affect the school's mission and objectives. Thus curriculum includes not only specific subjects in school but also activities students engage in at school and on their way to and from school.

Curriculum is ever-evolving. Teachers are expected to implement it, and principals are expected to supervise it. Certainly you can't be expected to

Effective Teachers	Effective Supervisors
- prepare their lessons well	- prepare their interactions with teachers well
- understand how each student learns	- understand how each teacher teaches
- understand how each student is motivated to learn	- understand how each teacher is best motivated to improve classroom, instruction and student learning
- encourage and facilitate student participation in the lesson	- facilitate teacher participation in the supervision process
- improve student learning	-improve teachers' instructional practices

Figure 2.1

be knowledgeable in every subject matter, yet you are expected to analyze teaching throughout the curriculum. You must take the lead in developing and nurturing rapport with teachers to better facilitate improved instruction and student achievement.

Consider this example. Several years ago a group of college professors visited Wales on an exchange. I stayed at the house of a former elementary principal who was now a professor at University of Swansea teaching methods courses and supervising elementary student teachers. We spent most of the first day discussing and comparing our respective teaching philosophies. After dinner that evening he mentioned he had to visit several student teachers the next day. I asked if I could go with him to observe. He agreed.

One urban elementary school we visited was very small. This was the professor's second observation of the student teacher this semester. In the pre-observation they reviewed her lesson plan. She was teaching Welsh, and the entire lesson would be in Welsh! Entering her room, we saw wall-to-wall kids and had to stand in a back corner to observe.

Now, I don't know the Welsh language, yet I felt comfortable enough to work FIAS and Teacher Question Index on the lesson. At home that evening we compared observations—his narrative and my data-driven FIAS and question index. Our observations were remarkably similar!

I then interviewed him on audiotape and typed our comparative observations and interview on his computer. The next day he and I reviewed and edited it, and I re-edited after returning from my trip. The article, "Student Teaching Supervision: A Cross Cultural Dialogue," was published in *Action in Teacher Education*, the journal of the Association of Teacher Educators.

iii. Instructional Theory

Knowledge of instructional theory is helpful in improving instruction. It can make or break a lesson. Throughout all supervisory interactions, a principal can use instructional theories as models, continually building rapport with teachers and teaching them to build and nurture rapport with students. One of the first instructional theorists, Robert Gagne, in his 1965 "Conditions of Learning" text, provided three theories of instruction:

- taxonomy of learning outcomes (similar to Bloom's taxonomy of cognitive, affective, and psychomotor outcomes)
- condition of learning
- events of instruction.

He also provided a structured and holistic view of teaching through his internal condition (what a student already knows) and external condition (what stimuli the teacher presents) rubric.

Should teachers be educational theorists? Yes, says Aleman (1992), who also feels they should know their own educational philosophy and what it is they're doing that makes them effective. According to Skinner, teachers fail because students' learning and teachers' teaching are not analyzed; thus, little or no effort is made to improve teaching as such (1968).

Analyzing actions by reflecting on our process of achieving them raises our awareness and helps us move from passivity to action (Wellington, 1991). Below are additional theoretical resources principals and teachers can access:

- theories of instruction (Gagne et al., 2004; Bruner, 1974; Rogers, 1994)
- teaching skills (Cooper, 2010; Philpott, 2009; Brophy & Good, 2007; Molnar & Zahorik, 1976)
- thinking skills (Kizlik, 2010; McGregor, 2007; Costa, 2001)
- dimensions of thinking (Marzano, 2006; Marzano et al., 1988)
- teaching styles (Moallem, 2007)
- approaches to teaching as cooperative learning (Palmer et al., 2003)
- brain-based learning (Jensen, 2008)
- models of teaching (Joyce & Weil, 2008)
- teaching with "dimensions of learning" (Marzano, 1992).

iv. Learning Theory and Styles

Learning theory tells us that not all students learn the same way. That's no surprise. There are many ways to learn and many ways teachers can encourage students to learn.

Learning styles are combinations of factors (cognitive, objective, psychomotor, environmental, personality, behavior, etc.) involving auditory, visual, and kinesthetic. Some students learn best with concrete examples, while others prefer abstract. Some students process actively, others process reflectively, and some use combinations. Principals and teachers should be aware of different learning styles that best accommodate students' learning needs; however, they must not overly depend on them. *The basic idea is, don't box a student in.*

Consider this example: A middle school teacher who, during the pre-observation conference of her first clinical supervision cycle, related her frustration about a specific student. "If I could ever get Jerry to pay attention," she said, "I'd drop over dead from the shock." As the principal videotaped her lesson, he noticed Jerry excitingly waving his hand, hoping to be called on to answer a question. Several times the principal zoomed the camera in on Jerry.

During the conference, the principal played the tape for the teacher. Amazed to see Jerry with his hand up, she looked at him and said, *"Where the hell did you get that?"* During the remainder of the conference, she still wouldn't believe that Jerry raised his hand. SHE DIDN'T SEE IT while she was teaching the lesson.

Unfortunately some teachers see a sea of faces rather than a student's face when they are teaching. That's sad. How long might it take students to figure this out? You already know the answer. With objective data from videotape, FIAS, or other tools we can help change that behavior, help improve instruction, and thereby help students achieve.

v. Motivation Theory

Motivation is either an internal or external force that helps satisfy needs or achieve goals. Some professionals say it is internal (intrinsic) and insist that you can "stimulate" but not "motivate" others by encouraging and inspiring. Others see motivation as external (extrinsic) and believe that you *can* motivate someone. Irrespective of semantics, motivation gives direction and intensity to behavior. There are (at least) five ways to look at student motivation:

- characteristics of the learner
- student interest in the topic
- available curriculum materials
- characteristics of the teacher, and
- instructional methods teachers use.

Equally important is motivation of teachers to perform effectively. Positive classroom changes call for the teacher's "intrinsic motivation" to make lessons exciting, meaningful, and lifelike.

Through both content and process theory, motivational theory stresses the need for, and importance of, motivation. It also stresses varied roles motivation plays in promoting more student interaction and willingness to learn, and more teacher willingness to improve instruction and grow professionally.

In motivation content theory, Abraham Maslow's hierarchy of needs, Douglas McGregor's Theory X and Theory Y (an extension of Maslow's ideas), Chris Argyris's immaturity-maturity continuum, and Rensis Likert's four systems of organization all provide numerous concepts for working more effectively with both students and teachers.

In motivation process theory, Leon Festinger's cognitive dissonance, Stacy Adams's social inequity, and Edwin A. Locke's goal achievement are useful. In behavior modification concepts, consider Fred Luthans and Robert Kreitner's reinforcement theory.

In the 1976 "clinical supervision" theme issue of the *Journal of Research and Development in Education*, Jack Frymier (Ohio State professor, ASCD president, and Education Honorary Kappa Delta Pi consultant) contributed a powerful, beautifully simple article on motivation in which he stressed that processes determine outcomes, and inputs determine processes. To improve the outcome (student learning), he said we must change either inputs or processes or both. But there are certain inputs we cannot change, such as STUDENTS (i.e., we get what we get). Frymier offered the model shown in figure 2.2:

Inputs	*Processes*
Students	Interactions
Teachers	Relationships
Administrators	Combinations
Curriculum	
Materials	Sequences
Time	Pressures
Money	Supports
Enthusiasm	Methods

Figure 2.2

In this and other content and process efforts, change begins with and remains the principal's responsibility. *Can there be any doubt about rapport's importance in motivation?*

C. RAPPORT PROCESS

vi. Positive Self-Concept

Every school experience students have affects their self-concept. When students feel good about themselves and their teacher, and have confidence in their abilities, they are more likely to succeed. Recognizing that their students' success or failure is as deeply rooted in self-concept as it is in measurable "intelligence tests," effective teachers treat their students accordingly.

Principals need to feel good about themselves too. To feel good about self, successful principals must have a good self-image built on strength and conviction. See the composite of your value system (strengths, weaknesses, abilities, and attitudes) and how they influence your interactions with others. You'll be able to garner further strength from them.

vii. Acceptance of Self and Others

Next is accepting one's self. Self-knowledge says the better I understand "me" the better my chances are of accepting "me" as I am. When I better accept myself, I become more open, can better perceive my abilities, and set realistic, achievable goals. The process of viewing myself positively, assessing myself more accurately through acceptance and openness, and better setting and realizing realistic goals helps me guide others through the same process.

If you don't accept yourself for who you are, how can others accept you? Successful principals must know that accepting themselves as they are helps them to better accept others for what they are and can do. Your self-confidence is projected to others through your persona, interactions, and professionalism.

viii. Communication

Without effective communication, rapport is not possible. An open communication atmosphere allows for confident interaction without fear. When it exists, everyone feels freer to express themselves, the stress of anxiety and pressure is lessened, and the rapport relationship is enhanced. All that leads to better teaching. These principles determine the effectiveness of principals' communication:

- *Be genuine*
- *Listen*

- *Talk with, not to, others*
- *Send congruent messages*

a. Be Genuine

Rapport begins by getting to know your colleagues and letting them get to know you. Start by trying to communicate warmth, openness, and sincerity. Show genuine interest in teachers' background, philosophy, interests, aspirations, strengths, and the like. Be humanistic by sharing some of your own interests and common experiences as well. But don't overdo talking about yourself. While personal examples serve a purpose, remember the main focus is the teacher. Establishing positive relationships necessitates building a foundation from which trust can grow. Is there a best way? Yes. Be genuine. Say what you mean and mean what you say.

b. Listen

Listening may be the most important skill a principal can possess. Allowing teachers to see you as a team member promotes collegiality. Accept and respect teachers for who they are and what they say. They need to know that you will listen with an open mind. They need to feel comfortable and secure in discussing their teaching concerns with you. Providing them with encouraging feedback allows them to feel good about themselves and their successes in teaching. Further, providing encouraging feedback will allow them to feel good about you.

c. Talk With, Not To, Others

Talk with, not to, teachers. Teacher anxiety toward classroom observation is normal. Replacing anxiety with comfort and respect is your job. Respect and vulnerability are two-way streets. *Before teachers will respect you, you need to respect them and they have to feel that respect.* Yes, you work hard to get teachers to respect you, but you must work even harder to show respect for the teachers.

Teachers feel vulnerable, but you as principal and teacher of teachers are more vulnerable—yet you have to be careful about how you express that to teachers. Do it in such a manner that you do not jeopardize the mutual comfort and respect already achieved. Yes, you are the school leader and student achievement is your responsibility. But you can't do it by yourself. You need the teachers' expertise. Talking with each other, allowing for open expression of ideas, questions, and concerns enhances positive self-images and promotes a comfort zone of trust that is conducive to achieving workable goals.

Several years ago, I supervised two very good second grade teachers in a team teaching situation. However, on this particular day, they did not do a good job. When they viewed their videotape in the conference, I asked how they thought they did. They said great. But it wasn't great. It was just the opposite. What to do? I sort of stalled, since it was getting late and they wanted to go home. I asked them if we could continue the discussion tomorrow. They said okay.

When we met the next day, they said, "Bob, we have to say something. We heard that you intended to fire a teacher and we didn't want that to be either one of us. We didn't sleep much last night. We stayed up talking to our husbands a long time and finally decided that because of the way you interacted with us yesterday it wasn't possible that you intended to fire someone. So we're ready to talk about yesterday's teaching."

Had I not done what I did yesterday, my supervision efforts with these two teachers would have been for naught. Further, word would have gone around quickly and all my supervision efforts with the other teachers probably would have been shot also. So be genuine. That works best in the long run.

d. Send Congruent Messages

Just as teachers need to send congruent messages to students, so too must principals send congruent messages to teachers. What you say influences teachers' perceptions and actions. If you send perceived incongruent, inconsistent verbal or nonverbal messages, you confuse the teacher, and their resulting interactions with students will likewise be affected.

Remember Jerry? He tried hard, but for some reason the teacher blocked him out. She couldn't/wouldn't see him paying attention. She couldn't/wouldn't see him succeeding. From time to time, all of us may be guilty of that type of behavior. We constantly send a message to others, be it verbal, nonverbal, or written. Unfortunately we are not always aware of how our messages are perceived, or whether one form of our message conflicts with another. Conflicting messages damage rapport. Thus, we need to concentrate on sending congruent messages.

Consider this example. A doctoral student/high school principal asked, "What can I do about teacher 'A'? For the past three years, she's been undermining me, trying to block most everything I do. I don't know how to handle it." His professor asked him if he tried talking with her. He said no. His professor suggested he try. He did.

The next time they met, he thanked his professor and relayed this scenario. "When I asked her why she was doing this, she replied that in a faculty meeting three years ago, I said something negative about her that both hurt and angered her. I was dumbfounded because I never thought I said anything negative about her, nor would I intend to. So our three years of rapportless relationship was built on a perceived noncongruent message from me."

Examples like this happen frequently. Why? Because sometimes teachers hear what they want to hear and students do too. *We can't underestimate the importance of congruent messages we send.*

ix. Evolving Learning of Subject Content

Irrespective of your specific content knowledge, it is important to feel comfortable supervising teachers in any content area. *Teaching is teaching, no matter the subject.* While some may challenge this statement, it is nonetheless true because good teaching principles are applicable in all subjects. *Similarly, supervision is supervision no matter the subject* and no matter your expertise in that specific subject. *That should not affect your ability to supervise!*

On the other hand, if you have expert knowledge in a specific subject, it can be beneficial to your supervising a teacher in that subject. Yet, you cannot let your subject expertise affect your supervising teachers in that subject. If you were a former teacher of that subject, don't let your perspective influence the teacher's teaching style. On the other hand, if you have little knowledge about a specific subject, you can use the teacher's lesson plans and frequent classroom visits to learn more about the subject.

Remember the example we discussed earlier about a professor visiting a foreign country and working with a former principal who became a university supervisor of student teachers. The visiting professor accompanied the supervisor to observe a student teacher teaching the country's language for which the visiting professor had no knowledge. When the visiting professor and university supervisor later conferred about the teaching they observed, their respective analyses and conclusions were almost the same. As principal you should not be reluctant to observe any teacher in any subject at your school.

x. Moxie

Moxie is being able to confront difficulties with fortitude and on-the-spot critical thinking. It stems from your confidence, expertise, healthy risk taking, and so on, and it seeks to address a crisis immediately and effectively. In your supervisory role, moxie is important for having courage to approach an unknown territory and execute a certain task.

If you supervise a new teacher you'll need to step outside your comfort zone and use the new environment as a learning opportunity for both yourself and the teacher. If you supervise teachers who have many years of teaching experience, you'll need moxie. Then again, if you supervise teachers approximately your age, that may be your biggest challenge, and you'll definitely need moxie. Remember that clinical supervision is systematic yet flexible. You may have to incorporate both in your supervisory interaction with teachers.

SUMMARY

Rapport is a harmonious relationship between people. It comprises both content and process—the why and how. Once established, rapport requires constant nurturing. Knowledge of content and process helps principals nurture rapport. Acceptance of self and others and knowing and practicing communication are two critical factors in principals' working to provide better supervision and clinical supervision. The key is genuineness, and listening is the most important skill.

FAQS

Does one need to know both rapport content and process? Absolutely.
Why? Because both content and process are rapport's foundation.
How did you determine rapport content and process? Through more than four decades of working with clinical supervision, I discovered that rapport is its foundation. Gradually, working with staff development and my graduate students, I was able to delineate both the content and process as presented in this chapter.
Why the stress on moxie? It brings common sense into the picture.
Are you saying that supervision is part of rapport content? Yes, a principal needs to be a continual exemplar of learning, and therefore must understand the whats and whys of supervision. That's a crucial mindset.
What about curriculum—same thing? Yes, although a principal does not need to be an expert in each subject, currency is important because curriculum is ever-evolving.
Why did you include motivation theory in rapport content? Because of its importance. Remember Jack Frymier's statement regarding the difference between motivation in schools versus motivation in product formation. He said that in production, the input is controlled. It is a known and steady entity.

In education we do not have that luxury. In schools, the input = students. Students vary in many ways. Thus schools don't begin with a steady input;

yet they are expected to form a final product. That's almost impossible. Throughout, teachers need all the objective/humane help principals can afford.

What is the most important part of the rapport process? That's a tough one because all are important. I've highlighted communication and vulnerability. The teacher may feel vulnerable in the objective analysis/clinical supervision process. The principal must continually work on reducing that vulnerability.

Equally important, or maybe even more so, the principal is vulnerable. That vulnerability must be communicated to the teachers by using all the rapport skills you can muster. How? By demonstrating your knowledge base in the most humane yet confident manner.

Example: A young principal was working with an experienced teacher who said, "I've been teaching longer than you were born." Moxie time. The principal thought for several seconds and then said, "Okay, now can we take a look at the data from the instrument?" Through conferencing with the teacher and using a genteel approach, the teacher soon came to realize that the principal knew his stuff. The teacher became one of the most ardent supporters of the process.

Section II

INTRODUCTION

This second section of *The Principal's Guide to Instructional Improvement: Theory to Practice* offers principals a deeper, user-friendly understanding of clinical supervision theory and practice, as well as self-taught skills to implement it in their own schools. While continuing to stress the importance of rapport as the mainstay of the clinical supervision process, this section further recommends that principals acquire a knowledge base of instruction analysis in order to completely maximize the long-term benefits of school supervision. Providing principals the opportunity to self-teach and experiment with the necessary skills, section II will provide principals with the confidence and experience required for improving school supervision and class instruction.

Because supervision is a long-term process, the final chapter offers a new, flexible instructional improvement model that emphasizes growth and not evaluation. This is achieved by a thorough explanation of the clinical supervision model that allows principals to choose from six tools to objectively analyze instruction: microteaching; Flanders Interaction Analysis; Behavior-Based Observation; Teacher Question Index; Teacher Index +; and videotaping.

Practice needs theory, and theory needs practice. Together, both sections will provide both.

Chapter Three

Clinical Supervision

In his landmark 1969 book, Bob Goldhammer stated:

> In its present stage of development, the clinical supervision that our minds can formulate and which we practice does not completely fulfill the ideology that occupies our imaginations.

Goldhammer was right. Why? Historically, supervision was hierarchical, inspection oriented, and highly evaluative. Objective instrumentation never entered the picture. Both teacher training and administrative/supervisory were poor. As a result, either intentionally or unintentionally, those who were placed in the supervisor role had to focus more on themselves than on the teaching; that is, "I like the way you did this . . . I think you should focus on the following, etc." That shouldn't be, because:

- it damages rapport, and
- it doesn't provide objective data on the teacher's performance.

When Harvard introduced clinical supervision in the latter 1950s, objective instrumentation was still noticeably absent. Passionate dreamers like Goldhammer wanted to take clinical supervision out of its infant stage of development, and their frustrations were evident. He envisioned more humaneness in the process and was anxious to see it happen. But it wasn't to be. The gaps remained unfilled.

The theme of the winter 1976 *Journal of Research and Development in Education* was clinical supervision. The preface hinted at some of the same frustration.

Conceived at Harvard, clinical supervision still remains primarily a latent force for the improvement of instruction. Written about, discussed, taught, and sometimes attempted, clinical supervision has yet to be fully born to the world of public education, K–12. Scholars and practitioners alike have made valiant efforts to stimulate its birth, yet clinical supervision remains largely in the womb. Perhaps, though, and hopefully so, its promised emergence is near.

In 2012, clinical supervision remains somewhat latent. Although some educators write about it and there are some present spinoffs, clinical supervision is not widely used. Why? Because it requires a knowledge base seldom offered to principals either in their preparation programs or in staff development. Clinical supervision is both concept and process. Concept is its most fundamental aspect because it provides process objectives. "Supervision" can evoke some fear in teachers. Adding "clinical" increases that fear.

By explaining the concept to teachers, principals can lessen that fear via rapport and by assuring teachers that clinical supervision is not meant to evaluate them! It was *never meant to evaluate teachers.* Rather, the process measures and analyzes teacher-student interaction through objective instrumentation. Then explain that its goal is twofold:

- instructional improvement for teachers, and
- collegial growth for both teacher and principal.

The purpose of using instrumentation, as we will describe in chapter 4, is to provide the teacher timely and useful data regarding what they actually did in class. Keep in mind, however, that the person using an instrument is more important than the instrument itself. Is that contradictory? No. You should have enough moxie to know which data you'll provide the teacher and enough skill to know how, when, and if you will provide that data to the teacher—keeping in mind that it is better to underwhelm than to overwhelm. Supervision is long term, not short term.

Again remind yourself that rapport is a mainstay in clinical supervision. As principal, you know that the only way that any type of supervision will work well as a long-term process is through your humane interaction with teachers, and you do that concentrating on and using rapport.

The clinical supervision techniques provided below will equip you with the necessary skills to successfully supervise teachers at any level. Generally, secondary teachers are more committed to content, and elementary teachers are more committed to process. Both, however, may show initial reluctance to clinical supervision. Your job is to minimize their reluctance. How? First, recall the six characteristics of clinical supervision listed in chapter 1. Second, be sure you understand them well enough to help teachers understand them. At this point, remind yourself of what we said before—that clinical supervision:

- is a deliberate intervention into the instructional process. You need to get that out into the open as soon as possible—but gently.
- is a goal-oriented, objective, yet flexible method to improve instruction. To achieve it, mutually establish growth plans with targets, timeline, and progress checks. Mutual is the key here, and you need to model that.
- assumes that you are competent in analyzing instruction. This and the following chapter provide you those skills. *Always assume that every teacher you work with is willing to improve instruction.* That's key, and your attitude will convince teachers.
- assumes a professional working relationship between teachers and you. That's your responsibility.
- requires a high degree of mutual trust, such as understanding, support, and commitment to growth of all involved.
- is a technology and uses technology for improving instruction. Two things are crucial:
  1. You are technology.
  2. You use technology (video recording, instrumentation, etc.) in clinical supervision.
  Keep reminding yourself, though, *you are more important than technology. Use technology and don't let it use you.*

You need to provide teachers sufficient staff development in understanding and accepting these six characteristics *before* you explain the clinical supervision model to them. Chapter 4 will provide you enough foundation to be effective in such staff development.

One last note. Clinical supervision does not have to be a one-to-one situation. Sometimes it is more effective when you work with several teachers at once. Why? Even with the positive rapport you establish, some teachers may still feel intimidated by clinical supervision. As noted earlier, supervision may make them nervous, and clinical supervision even more so.

If you work with two or three teachers at once, the power of clinical supervision comes in during the observation and conference. A self-conscious teacher may think, "I'm the only one with a specific behavior." As the other teacher(s) view the tape, they realize they have some of the same behavior. They'll become semisupervisors and reinforce (when pausing the tape) the teacher observed. The focus transfers from you to the instrument data and the teachers' interaction. The formula of one supervisor–several teachers, as in the example of the teachers who team taught, can be very powerful.

A. CLINICAL SUPERVISION MODEL

Recall the clinical supervision model presented in chapter 1. After you provide staff development in the six characteristics, you are ready to explain the clinical supervision model to teachers. Please remember the importance of developing and maintaining rapport in each step (see figure 3.1).

i. Pre-Pre-Observation

The pre-pre-observation can be casual or official via face-to-face, e-mail, or telephone. Its main purpose is twofold:

• ask the teacher when he would like to be observed, and
• ask the teacher to bring that lesson plan to the pre-observation conference, including objectives and how the lesson fits in their current unit of study.

ii. Pre-Observation

In the pre-observation, cooperatively confirm the time (as related in the pre-pre-observation), place, and method of observation. Ask the teacher to explain the lesson's objectives and instructional strategies to meet those objectives. Then collaboratively determine the observation focus. Focus range may include salient teaching patterns, student behavior/discipline, questions, reinforcement, delivery pace, teacher centeredness, student centeredness, nonverbal—either teacher or students, teacher movement patterns, teacher attitude, tech use, etc.

```
                              R
      Pre-Pre-Observation        A
      Pre-Observation             P
      Observation                  P
      Analysis & Strategy           O
      Conference                     R
                                      T
```

Figure 3.1

Suppose, though, the teacher has some reservation about being observed and wants you to focus on something you know they already do well. You would rather have the focus be on something else. What are you going to do? You have two choices. If you have good rapport with the teacher, you could softly and in a timely way suggest the focus be (that) something else. But if you feel pressing the issue would affect rapport, agree to the teacher's desired focus, knowing that the conference may eventually lead to (the) something else.

Be sure to reaffirm when (and where) the teacher would like to be observed. Then cooperatively determine details such as:

- what objective analysis instrument(s) you'll use and why. This text provides you the most researched, user-friendly, good interpretation/results instruments.
- when and how you enter the classroom, and how long you'll stay;
- where you will sit and what you will be doing during the lesson;
- who explains to students the purpose of your visit, and when. The teacher? Example—teacher asks students to be on their best behavior. You visit, and when teacher asks questions, he gets only silence. After you leave, students say to teacher—"see how good we were." Example—you explain to students at the beginning of class, by saying "I'm here to observe your teacher for a self-improvement project." A student may say, "Boy, you sure came to the right place." That may reduce both student and teacher tension.
- whether or not you should talk to the students during or after the lesson;
- when and how you'll exit the classroom; and
- when and where you'll conference regarding the observation.

Suggestion: Use a simple lesson plan format to include precise objectives (maximum two), time-flexible strategies, and probably five or six *key* questions. Also suggest teachers prepare a 3 × 5 card with about *ten praise words* appropriate to the age level of students they teach, tape it to their desk, and refer to it from time to time. Why? Good teaching revolves around asking questions—what, how, when, to whom—and how the teacher responds to students' answers. The suggested format is shown in figure 3.2.

iii. Observation

Remember, no surprises. That's crucial. When you observe, conform to the pre-observation agreements. Observe objectively with agreed-upon instrument(s) and be as minimally distracting to students and teacher as possible. When you're in classrooms a lot, the teacher and students will feel

Objectives (two maximum, in precise terms):

_____
_____
_____
_____

Teaching Strategies (including tentative time for each activity):

_____
_____
_____
_____

Key Questions (minimum 5, and 10 praise-words to use):

_____
_____
_____
_____

Teaching Materials (including when and how they will be used):

_____
_____
_____
_____

Self-Evaluation (completed within an appropriate time-frame):

_____
_____
_____
_____

Notes:

Figure 3.2.   Lesson Plan

comfortable and not notice you're there. They'll just go on with the lesson. That's your goal.

Suppose, however, that some of the teacher's behaviors are outside the boundaries of the focus and/or agreed-upon instrumentation. What do you do? Remain focused on your agreements but also record the other behaviors somehow. In the analysis and strategy step, you can decide whether or not (and how) to include these behaviors in the conference. Moxie! If the teacher has a behavior over which he has no control, don't bring it up in the conference. Supervision is a long-term process. Maybe somewhere down the line, you both can deal with it.

iv. Analysis and Strategy

In the analysis, use instrument(s) data to reconstruct the lesson as objectively as possible according to predetermined foci. You should have more than enough data. Sort and set the data into a usable and communicable form. *Saliency is the key* as you review the important and relevant foci behaviors— both those that are noticeably present and important and those that are noticeably absent *but should be there.*

Both analysis and strategy are included in this step of the model. Why? Because as you analyze, you're also thinking about how to present this data (how much and when) to the teacher in the conference.

As you develop a strategy, keep in mind two things:

• Concentrate on the foci, especially something you know the teacher can improve.
• *(In the conference) be sure to underwhelm, don't overwhelm.*

Supervision is a long-term process. Concentrating on one focus, or maybe two foci, the teacher can improve is doable. Improvement requires willingness of the teacher and consistent support from you. The better the teacher perceives your interaction and support, the more likely he is to improve and build on his teaching strengths. As creatures of habit, it has taken us a long time to perfect some habits—both good and bad. Supervision deals with people's values and perhaps involves changing certain habits. That's not easy.

It is always a good idea to *prepare several conference strategies*, thinking about possible consequences of each strategy. You can begin a conference by:

• asking the teacher to reconstruct the lesson you observed;
• stating the good things the teacher did in teaching that lesson;
• asking the teacher how she felt about the lesson; or
• stating what behaviors the teacher needs to improve.

Example: Suppose the lesson did not go well. If your only strategy is to begin the conference by asking how the teacher felt about the lesson and the teacher says, "I thought it went great," you're doomed. You may as well stop the conference right then! The teacher may be acting defensively or may actually feel that the lesson went well. But since you've not thought of an alternative strategy, there's nowhere for you to go. So develop several conference strategies.

v. Conference

Conference is a two-way street intended for teacher and principal growth. As you begin the conference, explore which strategy might be best to communicate effectively. Once you've established that, you can proceed. Eventually, you'll share treatable foci data in a timely fashion. It is important that both you and the teacher understand and accept your respective roles if the conference (and the entire clinical supervision process) is to succeed. That's your responsibility. Conferencing is tough. It will require your moxie skills and maybe even more.

Allow sufficient time between observation and conference. Immediate conferencing does not give you or the teacher adequate time to process the observed lesson. On the other hand, if you allow too much time between observation and conference, teacher anxiety may increase and perhaps negatively affect their current teaching. Try to conference within a week, and in the teacher's room rather than your office. Further, arranging either adjacent or side-by-side seating nurtures better rapport. Maintaining rapport is extremely important in the conference and beyond.

B. PRINCIPAL'S ROLE IN THE CONFERENCE AND BEYOND

- *Listen* to the teacher and be supportive.
- Concentrate on predetermined foci.
- Take an active (but not controlling) lead in the teaching analysis.
- Discuss and commit to a teaching improvement plan.
- Cooperatively determine an improvement timeline.

C. TEACHER'S ROLE IN THE CONFERENCE AND BEYOND

- Take an active role in the teaching analysis.
- Assume responsibility for improvement.
- Decide who will be involved in the improvement plan, and how.

- Commit to a teaching improvement plan.
- Cooperatively determine timeline for improvement and formative whole or partial clinical supervision sequences.

SUMMARY

In education, clinical supervision was created and developed by Morris Cogan and his colleagues at Harvard University in the 1950s. Collecting teaching data for the clinical process was primitive through scripting. Today, objective instruments are integral to collecting data.

Cogan viewed clinical supervision as an eight-step process. Robert Goldhammer, Cogan's doctoral student, simplified clinical into a five-stage process, emphasizing more of the human element. Ironically, Goldhammer's clinical supervision book was published in 1969, followed by Cogan's clinical supervision book four years later in 1973. Thus two camps were developed. In one were Cogan's followers and in the other, Goldhammer's followers.

Robert Anderson and I wrote the second and third editions of Goldhammer's book. I refined Goldhammer's model, emphasizing rapport throughout the process and also developed another model emphasizing data-driven instrumentation. Both are explained in this book.

Clinical supervision is more clearly defined than supervision. Teacher reluctance, however, remains. Principals are expected to be their school's instructional leader, yet principal training in clinical supervision aspects of instructional leadership is lacking in university preparation and staff development.

The advantage of clinical supervision is that principals can use it with any subject. The clinical supervision model included in this text provides principals with specific user-friendly details to self-teach the process.

FAQS

Why isn't clinical supervision used more in schools? There are several reasons.

- Very few universities offer clinical supervision courses in supervisor or principal preparation because faculty lack either the knowledge base or practical application.
- Very little staff development is offered for clinical supervision.

- Where training is offered, it is usually connected to or part of teacher evaluation.
- Clinical supervision was not designed for teacher evaluation.

Are teams always needed to conduct clinical supervision? No. In most cases, clinical supervision is one-on-one, but it is not limited to that model. A principal can work with several teachers at a time, and that can have great benefits.

Why? When several teachers are present in the conference, the observers can learn the system and can also learn more about their own teaching habits as they listen to the dialogue and join in.

Is clinical supervision difficult to learn? No. But I suggest you view and study its concept to better understand the process, because the concept provides process objectives.

As principal, how can I find time to conduct clinical supervision with all my teachers? My former colleague Bob Anderson was fond of saying that we carve out our job and do the things we feel most comfortable with. Principals sometimes find themselves in a catch-22 in that they are responsible for something but don't get training or support for doing it. I hope this text will allow you to be more comfortable with, and excited about, clinical supervision.

Can we use clinical supervision for teacher evaluation? Clinical supervision was not meant for evaluation but rather growth. Its beauty lies in the fact that both teacher and principal grow from the experience. If a teacher wants to include clinical supervision in her evaluation, you can—but only if the teacher initiates the suggestion.

Chapter Four

Instructional Improvement

Consider Chinese philosopher Lao-Tzu's 604 B.C. statement:

> A Leader is best
> When people barely know that he exists
> Not so good when people obey and acclaim him
> Worse when they despise him
> Fail to honor people
> They fail to honor you
> But of a good leader who talks little
> When his work is done, his aim fulfilled
> They will all say
> We did this ourselves

That's a timeless, wise principle that affects leadership success in most endeavors. Today's principals' success as instructional leaders is determined by how their teachers are stimulated to improve. Increasingly it will be determined by teachers being able to say, "We did this ourselves." Some sense of teacher ownership of both content and format of instructional improvement programs is crucial if we wish to succeed as instructional leaders. Is such leadership easy? No. Is it possible? Definitely; but there's no magic formula.

Revered ASCD leaders concur. In 1970, ASCD executive director Fred Wilhelms said, "What a supervisor is, is more important than what he does." Gordon Cawelti, his successor for 20 years, still believes that instructional improvement is the school's main goal. Further, he urges principals to spend at least half or more of their time in activities promoting instructional improvement. His successor and current ASCD executive director, Gene Carter, also stresses that dedicated, knowledgeable principals are needed to set the course for instructional improvement in schools.

Consider these examples:

1. In midsummer, a seven-year teacher unexpectedly became principal of a 300-student K-5 school in a rugged segregated housing area where few students knew their father. The old building's school yard was enclosed by a higher-than-normal chain-link fence. Playground equipment not cemented down was brought inside each night. She felt overwhelmed. Within her first year, though, she transformed the school into an instructional supervisor's dream as a model leader who fit Wilhelms' and Cawelti's description. She involved all teachers in planning and implementing instructional improvement, and she grew with them.

2. A recently (June 2011) retired Texas elementary principal of a high-turnover urban school where parents didn't value education also fit Wilhelms' and Cawelti's description. For more than fifteen years, instructional improvement was her priority. By managing time wisely, developing horizontal and vertical instructional teams, and delegating appropriately, she was able to observe classes a majority of each day. She transformed that school, restored pride, and won the respect of both students and parents. State and national awards for achievement became the norm.

3. An Atlanta high school principal was appointed midyear. The former principal, a twenty-year veteran at the school, was a top-down leader. The new principal tried to give the teachers some ownership. They didn't want it. Habits are hard to break. He backed off a little, then addressed instructional improvement by daily classroom visits until teachers were ready to trust his efforts.

4. A recently (also June 2011) retired Massachusetts small-town high school principal used similar tactics as the above 1. and 2. principals to enable him to observe in classrooms each day.

5. An Ohio elementary principal was always "around," around the teacher's lounge, around the hallways, and so on. His teachers readily said that they made all the decisions and he's just sort of "there." When I discussed the teachers' comments with him, he said—good, that's what I want them to say and believe. Yes, I'm here, there, "around," BUT I NEVER TAKE MY MIND OFF THE GOAL = student achievement.

6. A Beijing middle school principal works with his teachers to study and adjust the school philosophy every year—always concentrating on instructional improvement.

Exemplary Illinois, Wisconsin, Tennessee, South Carolina, and other school principal instructional leaders who fit Wilhelms' and Cawelti's descriptions also come to mind. Some have nice school buildings, some do not.

But buildings are not key, the person is. How are they successful instructional leaders? *Passion, keeping their mind on the goal, and respecting their teachers are common to all.* It's great to colleague with principals who have passion for improving instruction. And I'm assuming that all of you have these qualities too.

There is one more ingredient for leading instructional improvement—the knowledge base of analyzing teaching. This chapter illustrates the skills necessary to self-learn and use the instructional improvement model shown in figure 4.1. When you have a comfortable knowledge base of the model, you should feel confident enough to teach, demonstrate, and practice it with your teachers.

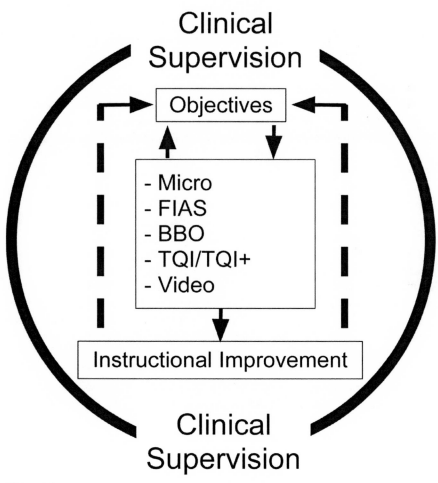

Figure 4.1

Clinical supervision embraces the entire instructional improvement model and is best accomplished when you use *objective* tools as:

1. Microteaching, a singular-focus mini-lesson with a teach/critique/reteach format.
2. Flanders Interaction Analysis System (FIAS), a social-psychological tool. It is the most researched and easiest teaching analysis system. It can be used with other tools also.
3. Behavior-Based Observation (BBO). Use it stand-alone or with FIAS.
4. Teacher Question Index (TQI). Use it stand-alone or with FIAS and/or BBO.
5. TQI+. Use it stand-alone or with FIAS.
6. Video. Use it to focus on and document specific classroom activities you and the teacher agreed upon in the pre-observation conference. It also provides a visual complement to any of the five objective tools listed above.

As the model shows, all instructional improvement begins with objectives. The model is cyclical. When you begin to use it, start with the teacher's lesson plan objective(s) [maximum two]. Together, you and the teacher determined in the pre-observation which objective instrument(s) you would use to analyze the lesson. You have the flexibility of using one, a combination of several, or all six tools.

If you decide to use microteaching, let the teacher teach a micro-lesson concentrating on a specific skill to ease the teacher's entry into clinical supervision. It is time-economical, safe, and relatively stress-free. Either peers or students form the mini-class.

Generally, though, you will observe the teacher's regular lesson in the classroom. With your guidance, you and the teacher choose which instrument(s) you'll use when you observe the lesson—FIAS, BBO, TQI, TQI+, video, or any combination of them, depending on the objective. If, after using your choice of these objective analysis tools, you and the teacher decide in the conference that the objective(s) are not met as well as you like, simply go back and restate objectives. Then start again, perhaps with a different choice of these objective tools you'll use.

As you successfully navigate through the clinical supervision model, you eventually arrive at instructional improvement. But you are not finished, because clinical supervision is a cyclical process. Always look for more improvement—that is, go back and establish new or revised objectives and start the process again. Suggestion: *use the full clinical supervision process not more than two times each academic year with each teacher.*

Though not mentioned in the model, as principal *you are both the foundation and implementing mechanism of the model.* Using the model is crucial. Why? Because it allows you to use objective tools. *You are the main clinical supervision tool and you also use tools. Keep in mind Wilhelm's statement about principals who dare to be instructional leaders—"what a supervisor is is more important than anything the supervisor does."* So always remind yourself:

- USE THE TOOLS WISELY—DO NOT LET THEM USE YOU, and
- YOU ARE MORE IMPORTANT THAN ANY TOOL.

The tools I include in this model are basic and should be easy for you to learn and use. Here we go!

A. MICROTEACHING

Microteaching was developed in 1963 by Dwight Allen and Bob Bush at Stanford University's Center for Research. Initially, it served three purposes:

1. train secondary teacher aspirants in selected skills;
2. research microteaching's value in teacher training; and
3. design in-service for teachers.

When Stanford's doctoral students secured positions at various research-oriented universities, they also used microteaching in their respective teacher education programs. Microteaching is still used in university teacher training programs.

As a five- to ten-minute teaching lesson concentrating on one observable skill, microteaching is a valuable clinical supervision asset. With it, teachers can experiment safely to obtain objective information on one of their teaching skills in a short time. Participants are a teacher, microclass (four to six students or peers), a video or audio recorder, and a supervisor (principal). The pattern is teach-critique, then reteach-critique with a new group of students or peers.

When the microteaching lesson is finished, students, recorder, and supervisor (principal) use videotape and other objective data to offer feedback and critique the lesson. Fortified with these suggestions, the teacher reteaches the lesson within a decided (short) time frame to a different group of students or peers. New students, recorder, and supervisor critique the new lesson, citing improvement for the focused skill.

Microteaching advantages are that it:

- is real teaching, simple and brief
- reduces teaching complexity to a specific skill practice as questioning techniques, praise, and so on, with specific length, and a small number of students or peers
- allows teachers to enhance and refine their skills in a safe environment
- allows for increase of control in a practice setting
- yields expanded supervisor, student immediate feedback.

You are expected to supervise every teacher in the school, many in curricular areas other than your own specialty. Microteaching is a good entry to clinical supervision. Here's how you can best and most efficiently teach and use microteaching.

- Select one of your better-skilled teachers as the microteacher.
- Choose someone to videotape and choose a recorder to take notes on the microteaching process.
- In pre-observation you and the microteacher decide the observable skill focus and review the lesson plan. Choose four or five teachers as students. Observe the lesson. Instruments used (in addition to videotape) depend on the skill to be observed.
- After the lesson, conference to provide feedback and critique the lesson, with everyone present—including students. Use the video to help. Pause it, reverse it, repeat parts, and so on, as necessary. Allow the microteacher plenty of input.
- After fifteen to twenty-five minutes, repeat the micro process with a new group of students or peers.
- You may decide to try this with just a small group of teacher observers at a time, or You can do it with a teacher and five peer/students, using your whole faculty as observers. That process further reduces teachers' anxiety and increases your rapport with them. Use the above method several times if you and the teachers wish. Supervision fears of all your teachers will diminish.

Those are two ways to begin your teacher staff development. Whichever you decide, it is important that both you and the teachers are at ease and will grow from the experience. Always remember, *do not use microteaching for teacher evaluation. Rather, this is a growth process for both you and teachers*. When teachers see you grow, they will too.

Example of how you can train teachers in both microteaching and clinical supervision:

Setting: October in an elementary school in Peter's first grade classroom. Peter has seven years' experience. Ruthann is a second-year principal with prior experience as an interim principal and as a teacher.

Pre-observation: The school's teachers are observing this process. Peter and Ruthann greet each other and then sit adjacently at his desk.

Peter: Hi Ruthann.

Ruthann: Hi Peter, how are you?

Peter: I'm fine, thank you.

Ruthann: And how is your son Jeremiah?

Peter: He's doing well, thank you. My wife Leah has arranged a job service for him, and a job coach helps him.

Ruthann: That's wonderful. You and Leah create such great experiences for him.

Peter: Thanks Ruthann.

(*Note how Ruthann concentrates on establishing rapport with Peter*)

Ruthann: Peter, I'm glad you volunteered to help demonstrate microteaching and clinical supervision to our faculty today—and allowing us to videotape it. Can we start with looking at your lesson plan?

Peter: Sure. [See figure 4.2.]

Ruthann: According to your objective and leading questions, I see you wish to experiment with grouping items.

Peter: Yes, I have a bag of items which I will empty out on the table. I will use questions to encourage students to see what types of groups they can physically arrange. It is a prelude to teaching set.

Ruthann: And what would you like me to focus on?

Peter: I'd like for you to focus on my questioning—whether it is open or closed, whether I use the appropriate level, and so on. Along with that, could you please observe whether my praise also encourages the students?

Ruthann: Well, okay, Peter. Generally we have one focus in microteaching, but in this case the two foci you chose go well together. So we can do that. (Ruthann asked for five volunteer teachers to play the role of first grade students, and five eagerly agreed).

Lesson Plan

Objectives(s): Students will have an elementary knowledge of set concept. Actually, students will be at the point of being ready to learn the specific set terminology at completion of today's lesson.

_____
_____
_____
_____

Procedure: A five minute lesson. I will begin with groups of items, then ask students how these may be grouped in different ways and why. The approach used will be that of discovery.

_____
_____
_____

Leading Questions: What do we have here on the table? How might we group these? What other ways are there of grouping these objects?

_____
_____
_____
_____

Materials for Teaching: Rubber bands, paper clips, pencils, pens, etc.

_____
_____

Other: table, chairs _____

_____
_____
_____
_____
_____

Self Evaluation: I'd like for the team to look at my questioning – open vs. closed. Also, I'd hope they look at whether I can use student ideas in bringing forth more ideas.

_____
_____
_____
_____
_____
_____

Figure 4.2. Lesson Plan

Observation: Peter began the five-minute lesson by greeting students, placing a bag on the table, then asking someone to empty its contents. In the bag, and now on the table, are five each of five items—rubber bands, paper clips, golf tees, ballpoint pens, and pencils. Peter asked students how they might group them, and students experimented. He used critical thinking questions to encourage them to arrange the items, praising them for each time they did. Soon the five minutes were up.

Analysis and Strategy: Ruthann, students, and observing teachers [Peter stays in the room and they pretend he is not there] discuss how Peter accomplished his objectives/foci and how Ruthann should conduct the conference. They reviewed the nature of his questions. Were they simple, complex, appropriate for grade level? Did he speak slowly enough, and did he wait for students to answer? Did he use sufficient and appropriate praise?

Conference:

Ruthann: Peter, can we begin with the videotape, and pause it when either you or I wish to point out a positive example of your focus effort?

Peter: Sure, I'd like that (and the conference continues, with analysis of Peter's questioning and praise and a few suggestions for Peter's next attempt at teaching the lesson to a different group of volunteer teachers).

The clinical supervision process repeats, skipping the pre-observation, and continuing with the remaining parts of the cycle.

Summary

Microteaching is a shortcut to instructional improvement. It is a real, scaled-down, singular-objective teaching sample in a safe venue. Five or six students are taught a five- to ten-minute lesson with the teacher focusing on improving one teaching skill. The lesson is analyzed by a supervisor (principal) and students, with suggestions for improvement. The cycle is repeated with five different students (or peers).

This concept is useful for you to use in supervising teachers. The principal becomes supervisor and trainer of teachers. In this microteaching training, five or six teachers are the students, the principal is supervisor and trainer, and the teacher is a volunteer teacher from the school. The training could be limited to those participants or to those participants plus the remaining teachers in the school. The latter probably is more efficient and effective.

FAQs

Can microteaching be real if five or six teachers are playing the role of, say, second-graders? Answer. You bet. I've used this method for decades and have seen many "real" situations. Picture, for example, an experienced teacher losing discipline three minutes into microteaching other teachers playing the role of x-graders. Her running behind the easel to cry, and the learning experience all of us received, including the microteacher, was superb. Hint: if a teacher cries, try not to let the teacher's tears dry up before you ask the teacher questions about the teaching. Is this technique harmful? No, because you ask questions, teacher answers, and the crying stops.

Why isn't microteaching used more? Microteaching was once an integral component of many teacher education programs. Some still use it. More important, I believe, is its use by the principal. Teachers are at once both trainees and trainers because they are intimately involved and have ownership in this process.

B. FLANDERS INTERACTION ANALYSIS SYSTEM (FIAS)

When former National Association of Secondary School Principal leader and ASCD executive director Fred Wilhelms said that supervision is the nervous system of the school, he added, "If I had just one tool with which to take the process of teaching apart to see what makes it tick—and thereby improve the process—that tool would be interaction analysis." He then said, "I have a hunch that administrators and teachers have hung back from using FIAS largely because they think it is a terribly complex and difficult process. Such fears are unjustified." Yes, Wilhelms was right. FIAS is one of the simplest and effective objective instruments to analyze instruction.

Interaction analysis systems date back to research on child development in the 1920s (when superintendents asked principals for help, and the principal organizations were formed). During the next thirty years, various scholars continued the analysis research. That research took a giant leap under the powerhouse University of Chicago professors in the 1940s and their soon-to-be significant scholar doctoral students. Former high school science teacher Ned Flanders was one of those students.

After completing his doctorate in 1949, Flanders spent five years at University of Minnesota (UMN) working on teacher and pupil talk categories. As a 1957 Fulbright Scholar in New Zealand, he began to refine categories and develop a "matrix." Sometimes important things are discovered at odd times and ways. He always liked to be near water. While looking at the water through his apartment window, he noticed the window panes. Aha! Matrix. Returning to UMN, he refined the system categories to ten and adjusted the matrix accordingly during the next three years.

Soon, doctoral students throughout the country were researching FIAS. Temple's Gertrude Moskowitz reveals first, *Flanders' 'rule of two-thirds'—2/3 of the time in class someone is talking, 2/3 of the time it's the teacher, and 2/3 of that time it is teacher direct influence.* Second, she notes, with the graphic picture of the matrix, you're your own change agent; you have 100 behavior combinations and patterns; you see yourself from the students' perspective. "I can look at myself objectively and admit to a matrix what I might admit to no man"; this has far-reaching powers even for daily personal relations; *"amazing what ten categories can do."*

In his Ohio State University dissertation, Richard Ober found that interaction analysis has great promise in bridging theory and practice. More important, he concluded that interaction analysis is not only useful as a supervisory tool, but it also allows a supervisor to be more specific and objective. FIAS provides meaningful and reliable feedback for teachers, showing that *indirect teacher behavior produces higher student achievement.* Why? It allows teachers to plan facilitative strategies and then sharpen skills to put those strategies into practice. Further, through practice, teachers can modify or revise strategies for more improvement.

Overall, research was consistent in noting that using FIAS made teachers more indirect. Distinguished researchers such as Edmund Amidon, Norma Furst, Anita Simon, Ernest Lohman, and Robert Soar all concluded that *interaction analysis makes teachers more aware of and more determined to be more indirect in their teaching to enhance more student involvement, attitude, and higher achievement.*

Thus far we know that FIAS, the most researched and easiest-to-use teaching analysis tool, focuses on teacher and student interaction in any subject classrooms. You can use it in microteaching, in a classroom of two students, or in a much larger classroom. I self-taught FIAS during my Duke University doctoral work, consulting with Flanders when I had questions. FIAS was key in my dissertation, and I continue to use it in K-graduate classes both here and abroad.

FIAS is a ten-category affective system that codes verbal action in three-second units of time. It is simple, as using it requires only one person. It works best when done live in the classroom, though you can use it via videotape as well. Its ten categories comprise indirect and direct teacher talk, student talk, and silence/confusion as illustrated in figure 4.3. Teacher talk has seven categories, student talk has two categories, and silence or confusion is the remaining category.

In teacher talk, the first four categories are indirect influence. The next three categories are direct teacher influence.

Category one of teacher indirect influence—accepting student feelings—seldom occurs in classroom interaction. When it does, it's usually after a student introduces a statement trying to get the teacher off-topic. Teacher response can either be close to praising, or criticizing. If the teacher accepts

		1. Accepts Feeling: accepts and clarifies the feelings of the students in a non-threatening manner. Feelings may be positive or negative.
Teacher Talk	**Indirect Influence**	2. PRAISES OR ENCOURAGES: Praises or encourages student action or behavior. Jokes that release tension, not at the expense of another individual, nodding head or saying "um hm?" or "go on" are included.
		3. ACCEPTS OR USES IDEAS OF STUDENTS: Clarifying building, or developing ideas suggested by a student. As a teacher brings more of his own ideas into play, shift to category five.
		4. ASKS QUESTIONS: asking a question about content or procedure with the intent that a student answer.
	Direct Influence	5. LECTURING: giving facts or opinions about content or procedure; expressing his own ideas, asking rhetorical questions.
		6. GIVING DIRECTIONS: directions, commands, or orders to which a student is expected to comply.
		7. CRITICIZING OR JUSTIFYING AUTHORITY: statements intended to change student behavior from nonacceptable to acceptable; bawling someone out; extreme self-reference.
Student Talk		8. STUDENT TALK-RESPONSE: a student makes a predictable response to a teacher. Teacher initiates the contact or solicits student statement and sets limits to what the student says.
		9. STUDENT TALK-INITIATION: talk by students which they initiate. Unpredictable statements in response to teacher. Shift from 8 to 9 as student introduces own ideas.
		10. SILENCE OR CONFUSION: pauses, short periods of silence and periods of confusion in which communications cannot be understood by the observer.

Figure 4.3.   Categories for The Flanders System of Interaction Analysis: Ned A. Flanders

*There is NO scale implied by these numbers. Each number is classificatory, it designates a particular kind of communication event. To write these numbers down during observation is to enumerate, not to judge a position on a scale.

the student's feelings verbally and gently gets back to the topic, that's good. Too much of students doing this, though, may cause the teacher to become frustrated and respond with criticism, as "okay, but pay attention to what we are doing."

Category two—praising and encouraging—is generally meant to be vocal praise, although some nonverbal actions, as teacher facial gestures, nodding, tapping student on the back, and so on, can be coded as a two as well.

Category three—accepting and using student ideas—usually occurs after a student responds to a teacher question.

Category four is asking a question—with the intent that a student answers. Categories four and six are similar. The easiest way to differentiate is—when teacher asks a question, then calls on a student, code a four (e.g., what's the answer to____, Johnny?). If the teacher calls on a student then asks the question, code a six (Johnny, what's the answer to____?). Do this with a caveat—always be consistent.

Teacher direct influence starts with category five—lecturing. That's self-explanatory.

Category six, giving directions, is self-explanatory too. As noted above, it can also occur when a teacher states the student's name before asking a question (e.g., Jimmy, what's the answer to _____?). When coding, always remember—be consistent. Classify four as a question, and classify six when the teacher calls on the student, then asks the question.

Category seven is criticizing. Teacher voice and attitude play a role. You also should code category seven when a teacher uses excessive self-reference.

Student talk has two categories, eight and nine. Category eight is student responding to a teacher question when called upon. Category nine is when a student answers a question without having been called upon, or when a student simply initiates a comment.

Category ten is silence or confusion. Although silence can be an effective teaching tool when the teacher is waiting for an answer to a question, confusion is not.

One of the great benefits of FIAS is that while some interaction analysis tools require multiple observers and/or recorders, FIAS requires only one observer—you. You can use FIAS either live or via videotape. Live is preferable.

Training Teachers in FIAS

When you intend to use and teach FIAS, first memorize the ten categories and ask the teachers to do the same. That's essential for accurate and efficient coding. Action takes place fast in the class and you have to code—without interpreting or thinking "I believe this is what the teacher meant." Why? You want to ensure objectivity as best you can.

Example: Suppose you were a math teacher before you became a principal. When you taught, you used certain strategies that worked well for you. Be cautious as you code in a math classroom. It is important that you code the teacher's behavior and strategy as it occurs and not think of how you taught your math class and try to get the teacher to do the same thing you did.

How and where do you code? Use a blank 8-1/2 × 11 sheet of paper. Code in columns, beginning on the left. Every three seconds write the number that corresponds to the category of (inter)action. Begin coding with ten at the top of the first column (and later at the bottom of the last column).

If you followed this procedure and coded every three seconds, you have twenty entries per minute. So for a twenty-minute coding period you would have 400 entries, and for a thirty-minute period of observing you would have 600 entries. That's a lot of data.

In coding, there are a few rules of exception. One is that *if more than one action occurs in a three-second interval, code each (vertically in column).*

Example: teacher asks, "what is 4 × 2?" Student answers "8." Teacher says, "8, that's right." In this three-second interval, four actions occurred—4 (teacher asked question "What is 4 × 2"?), 9 (student answered "8" without having been called upon), 3 (because teacher used/repeated student answer—"8"), then 2 (teacher praised student "that's right"). You record 4, 9, 3, 2 for that three-second interval. Do likewise for other examples of several interactions occurring within a three-second interval.

Code for 20 minutes. You will have about 200+ numbers. When the first column is exhausted, start a second column, and so on. Your coding will look like the example in figure 4.4 (a FIAS sixth grade reading).

The next step is to "pair" your coding numbers (see figure 4.5). Pair first number with second, then second with third, then third with fourth, etc., by using alternate parenthesis-like markings for each pair. When you get to the bottom of the first column, connect the last number of the first column with the first number of the second column. Do the same for each column. If you have 400 entries, you will have 399 pairs because the first number (10) and the last number (10) are used only once.

Using the above coding example, this is how to get those number pairs into a matrix.

You will work with two matrices, a tally matrix (see figure 4.6) and a finalized matrix (see figure 4.7). The tally matrix has larger cells to accommodate your tallies. Some cells will have a large number of tallies from the teacher-student interaction.

The finalized matrix has smaller cells because it just accommodates the number sum of tallies from respective cells of the tally matrix.

Tally number pairs from the sixth grade reading class. First use the tally matrix. Transfer pairs' tallies to the tally matrix. First pair = 10–8. On the tally matrix, start at the upper left corner, go down ten rows and over right eight columns, and insert a tally in the 10–8 cell. Second pair = 8–8. Go down eight rows, and over eight columns, insert a tally in 8–8 cell. Third pair = 8–2. Go down eight rows and over two columns, and insert a tally in 8–2 cell. Continue for all pairs.

Now total tallies in each cell of the tally matrix and transfer tally totals to respective cells of the finalized matrix.

The next step is to total each column of the finalized matrix. Column 1 has no entries = no accepting student feelings. Column 2, praising/encouraging, has twenty entries; that is, the teacher praised students twenty times. Likewise for column 3 = accepting ideas: the teacher used student ideas/repeated what student said twenty times. Total the remaining columns too. The total number of entries in columns 1–10 is 217. Given that total, this matrix is reporting

10	4	8	8	4	3	5
8	8	4	8	5	4	5
8	4	8	3	4	8	5
2	10	2	3	4	8	5
2	4	4	4	8	5	4
4	8	8	8	4	4	8
4	2	8	8	8	4	8
8	4	8	8	8	10	4
2	8	4	2	10	6	8
4	8	8	3	8	8	3
8	8	8	4	8	8	5
8	2	2	8	3	8	5
2	4	4	8	4	8	4
3	8	4	3	8	4	10
4	3	4	3	8	8	
10	4	4	3	8	8	
3	4	8	4	2	4	
3	4	8	8	4	8	
4	5	4	8	8	8	
10	5	8	2	8	3	
8	5	8	2	8	5	
2	5	2	5	2	5	
4	5	4	5	2	5	
8	5	10	3	4	5	
2	5	6	3	8	5	
3	6	6	5	8	5	
4	4	6	5	4	5	
8	4	5	4	8	6	
3	10	4	4	2	4	
4	10	10	8	8	8	
4	8	8	5	8	8	
6	8	8	5	8	2	
8	2	8	5	4	3	
8	4	8	4	8	3	

Figure 4.4.   Flanders Coding: 6th Grade Reading

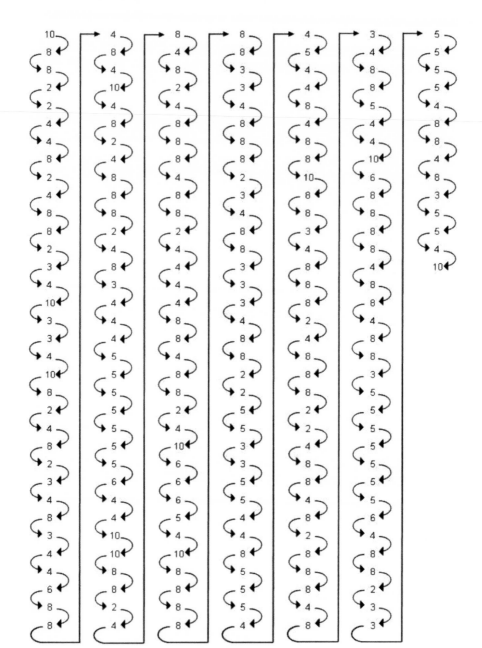

Figure 4.5. Flanders Pre-Matrix Tally: 6th Grade Reading

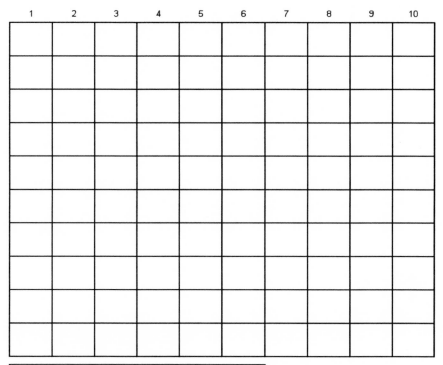

1	2	3	4	5	6	7	8	9	10

OBSERVATION CODES

1	Accepts Feeling
2	Praises or Encourages
3	Accepts Ideas
4	Asks Questions
5	Lectures
6	Gives Directions
7	Criticizes or Justifies Authority
8	Student Responds
9	Student Initiates
10	Silence or Confusion

Figure 4.6. Tally Matrix

twenty or twenty-one minutes of classroom interaction. Your finalized sixth grade reading matrix now looks like figure 4.8.

Before you begin interpreting the matrix, calculate four more items. First, teacher talk: add sums of the first seven columns, divide by total of all ten columns: 131 divided by 217 = 60 percent. Next, student talk: add sums of columns 8 and 9, divide by total of all columns: 76 divided by 217 = 35 percent. Third, silence or confusion: divide sum of column 10 by 217 =

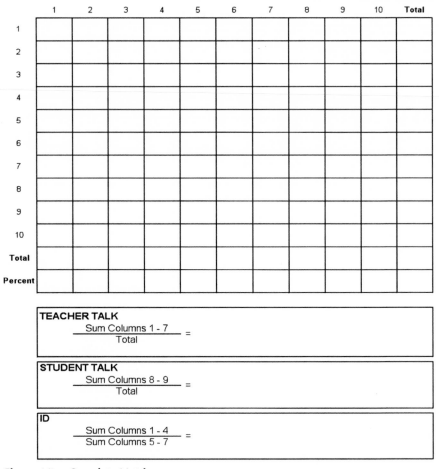

	1	2	3	4	5	6	7	8	9	10	**Total**
1											
2											
3											
4											
5											
6											
7											
8											
9											
10											
Total											
Percent											

TEACHER TALK
$$\frac{\text{Sum Columns 1 - 7}}{\text{Total}} =$$

STUDENT TALK
$$\frac{\text{Sum Columns 8 - 9}}{\text{Total}} =$$

ID
$$\frac{\text{Sum Columns 1 - 4}}{\text{Sum Columns 5 - 7}} =$$

Figure 4.7.   Complete Matrix

approximately 4.6 percent or round to 5 percent. Lastly, indirect teacher talk compared to direct teacher talk = ID ratio. Divide sum of columns 1 through 4 (indirect teacher talk) by sum of columns 5 through 7 (direct teacher talk): 94 divided by 37 = 2.5. That means the teacher was more than twice as indirect as direct.

So now, using the sixth grade reading coding and matrix you've taught the teachers how to code FIAS, how to prepare the tally matrix, how to transfer tally totals to the finalized matrix, and how to determine totals for columns, determine teacher and student talk and silence/confusion, and how to determine the ID ratio. Now you can begin to explain how to interpret the matrix.

	1	2	3	4	5	6	7	8	9	10	Total
1											
2		3	4	11	1			1			20
3			6	10	4						20
4				12	2	1		31		8	54
5			1	7	20	2					30
6				2	1	2		2			7
7											0
8		17	8	11	2			37		1	76
9											0
10			1	1		2		5		1	10
Total		20	20	54	30	7		76		10	217
Percent		9%	9%	25%	14%	3%		35%		5%	100%

TEACHER TALK

$$\frac{\text{Sum Columns 1 - 7}}{\text{Total}} = \frac{131}{217} = 60\%$$

STUDENT TALK

$$\frac{\text{Sum Columns 8 - 9}}{\text{Total}} = \frac{76}{217} = 35\%$$

ID

$$\frac{\text{Sum Columns 1 - 4}}{\text{Sum Columns 5 - 7}} = \frac{94}{37} = 2.5$$

Figure 4.8. Complete Matrix: 6th Grade Reading

When you use FIAS in the clinical supervision process and teachers understand how to transfer number pairs to the matrix, try this. After you observe the lesson and code the interaction in columns, give the teacher the columned page of numbers along with blank tally and finalized matrices. As teachers pair and transfer to tally and finalized matrix, they better understand their teaching patterns. When they come to the conference with a prepared matrix, your supervisory job is much easier. The focus is on the matrix DATA and less on you. You and the teacher can then work better collectively in analyzing the DATA matrix.

But remind yourself again, it is important how you use this tool.

a. Matrix Column Analysis

Continue to use the sixth grade reading matrix as a model from which to learn. When you explain the matrix, put a copy on the overhead, rather than letting teachers use handheld machines because it is easier to keep teachers focused and you can better answer their questions by using the large screen.

Every matrix has 100 cells, each with possible important interaction information revealed. *First, look at column totals.* Indirect teacher talk =columns 1–4 = how many times the teacher accepted feelings, praised, used student ideas, or asked questions. Direct teacher talk =columns 5–7 = how much the teacher lectured, gave directions, or criticized.

Student talk = columns 8–9 = how many times a student responded/answered questions when called on and how many times a student initiated talk to either the teacher or another student. Silence or confusion = column 10 = silence when people are thinking, and confusion—self-explanatory.

Next, teacher talk percent = sum of columns 1–7 divided by the sum of columns 1–10. Student talk percent = sum of columns 8–9 divided by sum of columns 1–10. Teacher's ID = indirect to direct ratio = sum of columns 1–4 divided by sum of columns 5–7.

All those percentages can be valuable and give you and the teacher a starting point for discussion.

When analyzing matrix columns, start by comparing column totals. Begin with columns 2 (praise) and 3 (use student ideas). Ideally, they are similar (they happen to be equal in our sixth grade reading matrix). If threes outweigh twos two to one, teacher is not praising enough. The teacher responds to a student's answer by using it, then either asking another question or going back into lecture (repeatedly). Students quickly know that (a) the teacher is not interested in their answer and (b) the teacher doesn't praise enough. Either way, students become less motivated or interested to answer future questions.

If twos outweigh threes by a factor, that may or may not be okay. The teacher may be using one praise word too much and not realize it. Students realize it, and some tally instead of following the lesson. That's teacher's fault. Example: Okay, class, we're going to, okay, do this today, okay? Okay. Then student answers a question, teacher says okay. Using okay as a sentence opening, comma, period, transition, and praise won't work. Students become less motivated or interested to answer future questions. *Good* is another example. Excessive repetition of question-answer-good, question-answer-good = robotic teaching, which can cause boredom and discipline problems.

Now look at the 4 column. Compare the fours with the sixes. Are there many sixes? The analysis is obvious. Fours are better than sixes because four means the teacher asks, whereas six means the teacher tells. Six may also indicate rhetorical questions, depending on teacher voice/mannerisms. Four times two is eight—RIGHT? The emphasis on *right* I used because after a teacher does this a few times, that RIGHT may become louder to the student. Who would want to answer that rhetorical question?

Looking at fives can be common sense or in rare cases depend on the lesson. Either way, too many fives are not good.

Looking at sevens—well, it is best not to have them. Sometimes it is necessary, but hopefully very few times.

Look at student talk totals for 8 (response) and 9 (initiation). If eights greatly outnumber nines, it usually means the teacher expects students to answer only when called on. It can reflect teacher direct behavior and discipline control, or maybe poor preparation. On the other hand, if there are too many nines, it may mean that the teacher is too laissez-faire. That may lead to chaos. In our sixth grade reading example, only eights appear; no nines. Just as with twos and threes, look for a healthy blend of eights and nines.

Look at silence/confusion. After many years of using FIAS, I've found that up to 10 percent may be okay, but that needs further analysis. More than 10 percent may indicate too much confusion. To better analyze tens, you may need to go back to the column pairs sheet. With each instance of 10, circle it and the number before and after it. Patterns emerge.

Compare teacher talk with student talk. Teacher talk = sum of columns 1–7 divided by total interactions. Student talk = sum of columns 8 and 9 divided by total interactions.

Determine teacher indirect to direct ratio. ID = sum of columns 1–4 divided by sum of columns 5–7. Hopefully it is greater than 1. Remember Flanders' 2/3 rule? Some teachers don't realize they talk too much. If a teacher says 25 percent, it could mean close to 50 percent. If a teacher says 50 percent, that's trouble. It could be 80 to 90 percent. If so, students seldom get a word in, or give a rote response to a rhetorical question like "4 × 2 = 8, right?" Some try to sneak in a word while the teacher is catching his breath. Neither situation is good. In the conference, don't fall into the same trap by doing all the talking!

Before explaining sequential analysis, consider the diagram shown in figure 4.9. If a teacher asks a question and a student answers, teacher response can be either 1 (accepts feeling—if student answer does not respond to the question), 2 (praise), 3 (use idea), 4 (another question), 5 (lecture), 6 (give direction), 7 (criticize). To keep away from the question-answer-good routine, suggest that the teacher write ten praise words appropriate to grade level, tape it to the desk, or keep it handy in some manner.

Other possibilities: Double praise 8-2-2 (great! That's super), 8-3-3-3-4 (continued use of student idea, followed by another question to expand the answer), or an 8-3-2 (use of idea followed by praise—you said xxxx, that's close), 8-4 (no praise or use of idea, but rather asking another question). That

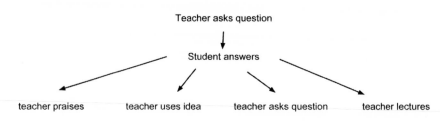

teacher accepts student feelings   teacher gives direction   teacher criticizes

Silence

Figure 4.9

can be good, but too much leads to students' not feeling appreciated. Eight-five also makes students feel unappreciated and indicates teacher control/domination. Eight-six (you already know what happens with that). Eight-seven (a no-no unless it is warranted). Eight-eight can mean more than a yes or no answer. Same is true for 9-9.

Since research and common sense say that indirect teacher talk leads to increased student involvement and achievement, variation seems appropriate—both verbal (including inflection) and non-verbal (smile, gestures, etc.). Example: explaining 8-2-2 (THAT's GREAT! [now in a soft voice] that's an excellent answer{ that will awaken even the best sleeper too = preventive discipline}) or an 8-2-3 and so on.(super, you said . . .). What about an 8-3-3 or an 8-3-2?

b. Matrix Sequential Analysis

FIAS column analysis affords important teaching data. Sequential analysis is more powerful since it reveals many teaching patterns. Example: you can discover a lot about a teacher's preparation and effectiveness by looking at teacher questions, what happens after a teacher asks a question, (if the teacher gets an answer) and what he does with the answer, how teacher praises which students, the type of questions teacher asks of whom, and so on. Used prop-

	1	2	3	4	5	6	7	8	9	10	Total
1											0
2		3	4	11	1			1			20
3			6	10	4						20
4				12	2	1		31		8	54
5			1	7	20	2					30
6				2	1	2		2			7
7											0
8		17	8	11	2			37		1	76
9											0
10			1	1		2		5		1	10
Total		20	20	54	30	7		76		10	217
Column Percent											

ID = 94/37 = 2.5

Teacher Talk	Student Talk
Columns 1-7	Columns 8-9
131/217 = 60 %	76/217 = 35%
% of total talk	% of total talk

Figure 4.8

erly, these data will be useful feedback for the teacher. Plus, it can help you gain more rapport with and respect from the teacher as you cooperatively work on an improvement plan.

Continue with the sixth grade reading matrix shown in figure 4.8. First, look at row 4 to determine question effectiveness. The teacher repeats/has long questions twelve times, starts to lecture twice, and gives students directions once after asking a question, perhaps indicating question preparation or skill. Thirty-one times students answer, but only when called on. No student initiation. Teacher control may be an issue. Eight times there is silence or confusion. Which?

Go to row 10. Once the teacher repeats a question after silence, and twice gives directions after silence. The five entries in the 10-8 cell may relate to the eight entries in the 4-10 cell, meaning that the student called on to answer may have thought before answering.

Go to row 8 to find out what happened after a student (who was called upon) answered the teacher. The teacher praised seventeen times—that's good—used student(s)' ideas eight times—okay, but that's a 2-1 ratio—asked another question eleven times [maybe not a good indicator], and twice went into lecture. The thirty-seven entry in the 8-8 cell means the student's answer was more than a yes or no—that can be good. What FIAS does not tell you, though, is how many students answered. I'll explain later how you can determine that.

There are no entries in row nine. That's understandable, but not good since the teacher did not allow students to answer/initiate without being called on.

Go to row 2. After the teacher praised student(s) [recall the seventeen entries in the 8-2 cell] she continued the praise three times [good], used the student(s)' idea four times, but went directly to another question eleven times [pattern may be question/answer/good, question/answer/good].

Go to row 3. Recall the numbers in the 8 row—eight uses of idea and thirty-seven continued answers. Six times the teacher used student ideas after student answered, but ten times the teacher immediately asked another question [maybe not good] and four times went into lecture [probably not the best].

Row 5 does not really offer that much for analysis.

Row 6 does not offer much for analysis either except possibly for the two entries in the 6-4 cell, i.e., tell then ask, and the two entries in the 6-6 cell, tell, tell. But those entries do not really say too much.

This lesson appears to be a review lesson. If that's true, the absence of student initiation can be better understood if the teacher is trying to help certain students. If it was not a review lesson, this appears to be a teacher-controlled class. The ID ratio, 2.5, may also be an indicator of a review lesson. The teacher offered praise and used student ideas, and questioned a lot. Without being in the class to observe, we don't have enough insight.

Explanation of how many students answered. When you code FIAS, you may also—after becoming proficient in coding—use alphabet or numbers to identify students. So when you code an 8 (student response) or 9 (student initiation), you place to the right of the 8 or 9 the code you selected for each student. Thus 8c means student c answered; or 84 means student 4 answered. Become proficient in coding, though, before you try subcoding. Why? You might miss some of the interaction.

To help you better understand sequential analysis,

• start by looking at row 4. Was questioning clean? Did students answer [4-8 cell or 4-9 cell] or did teacher repeat questions, lecture, or give directions [4, 5, 6 cells]?

- check rows 8 and 9 [student response, student initiation] to compare teacher praise and use of student ideas. Hopefully there is not a large difference between the two. While still in rows 8 and 9 check the 4, 5, and 6 cells [teacher asked another question, lectured, or gave a direction].
- check rows 2 and 3 [praise and use ideas]. Did the teacher continue praise [2 cell], use ideas [3 cell], or go to questions, lecture, or giving directions [4, 5, or 6 cells]?
- special note: If row 4 has many entries in 10 cell [silence or confusion], check row 10 right after checking row 4. Maybe you can determine what the teacher did after the silence, e.g., cell 2 = encourage student to answer, cell 4 = ask another question, cell 5 = lecture, etc.

Figure 4.10 shows a sample row 4—what happens after the teacher asks a question. She knows what and how to ask. Why? After asking, students answered, twenty-five in the 4-8 cell (response) and twenty in the 4-9 cell (initiation), and almost no entries in 4-4, 4-5, 4-6 cells (two in the 4-4 cell and one each in 5 and 6). Questions are clean—mostly student answers, and a good balance of student response and initiation.

Next example: Teacher drags out or repeats questions thirty-two times, goes into lecture fifteen times, and told a student to answer twenty-one times. She also criticized five times. Suppose many of the thirty-two entries were (probably) the teacher's restating a question several times, each time differently. Some students are still thinking about question one, some question two, etc. If teacher calls on a student who is still thinking about question one and answers accordingly, what is the teacher's response? Criticize or just ignore the student. Either way, the fault lies with the teacher. See figure 4.11.

Next example (see figure 4.12): Teacher asked a question, student answered [4-8 cell = 23]. What did she do then? Go to row 8. She praised eleven times (8-2 cell), used ideas twenty-one times (8-3 cell), asked another

	1	2	3	4	5	6	7	8	9	10
4				2	1	1		25	20	3

Figure 4.10

	1	2	3	4	5	6	7	8	9	10
4	1		2	32	15	21	5	16	12	21

Figure 4.11

question three times (8-4 cell), had twelve extended student answers (8-8 cell), two student initiations (8-9 cell), and two instances of silence or confusion. Teacher seems more comfortable using student ideas than praising.

Check row 9. Compare 8-2 cell and 9-2 cell, then 8-3 cell and 9-3 cell. Same pattern—she uses ideas more than she praises. (Variables as type of students, teacher experience, etc., are factors in every lesson). Note the 9-1 cell. Sometimes ones and twos are close behaviors.

Go to row 10. What happened after silence? Teacher repeated or asked another question fourteen times (10-4 cell). Well, so what? It may mean that teacher did not ask clearly, and rephrased. If that occurred regularly, teacher's questioning technique can be an issue.

Still in row 10, we see eleven instances of silence then lecture (10-5 cell), indicating poorly asked/phrased questions. After not getting an answer, four times teacher told another student to answer (10-6 cell). The 10-8 and 10-9 cells show students answer after silence. That's good. The 10-10 cell shows ten instances of silence followed by silence, nothing to be alarmed about if it indicates students thinking about an answer.

Case Study 1: Brenda has taught high school math at Bradenwood for eight years. You have been principal there for five years. You conduct clini-

	1	2	3	4	5	6	7	8	9	10
4	7			7	4	2		23	19	15

	1	2	3	4	5	6	7	8	9	10
8	1	11	21	3		1		12	2	2

	1	2	3	4	5	6	7	8	9	10
9	4	3	12	5		2	1		8	5

	1	2	3	4	5	6	7	8	9	10
10		2	1	14	11	4		5	11	10

Figure 4.12

	1	2	3	4	5	6	7	8	9	10	Total
1			1	1	1	1			2		
2		3	6	6		2		10	5	5	
3	2	5	5	31	6	13		2	9		
4		1	1	3	1			51	19	12	
5		2	1	7	15	4		7	1	3	
6		1	2	8	1	2	3	12	3	15	
7								2		2	
8	1	20	37	8	10	8		9	4	8	
9	3	1	19	14	1	8	1	1	2	7	
10		4	1	10	5	9		9	13	1	
Total	6	37	73	88	40	47	4	103	58	53	509
Column Percent											

ID = 204/91 = 2.24

Teacher Talk Columns	Student Talk Columns
1-7	8-9
57	31
% of total talk	% of total talk

Figure 4.13. Matrix A1: High School Math

cal supervision cycles with each teacher twice each year. You observe her in October = matrix A1 (see figure 4.13).

Pre-pre-observation: Informally you ask her when would be a good time for you to observe and remind her to bring a copy of her lesson plan to the pre-observation.

Pre-observation: During the conference you observe that her lesson plan looks good. Objectives are clear, strategies seem appropriate, and the four key questions should bring good answers. She asked you to focus on her questioning and her response to student answers. She thinks that she praises too much.

Observation: Several days ago she told the students when you would be observing. When you entered class, you took a seat at the back. You stayed the whole period, using FIAS and videotaping. Your policy on videotaping is to record by splices, about eight minutes total, concentrating on the focus.

Analysis/strategy: You completed matrix A1. In column analysis, she used six ones (okay), thirty-seven twos and seventy-three threes (a 1-2 ratio that you'll talk about in the conference). Questions were abundant (88), lecture was low (40), but directions seemed high (47), and she criticized four times. Student response (103) and initiation (58) show a 2-1 ratio—something you'll talk about, and in relation to the twos and threes. Silence/confusion = 53. She talked 57+ percent of the time and students talked 31 percent of the time. Her ID ratio was 2.24.

Sequentially, row 4 shows fifty-one answers by students called upon and nineteen responses via initiation; and there were twelve instances of silence. Checking row 8 (since she received fifty-one responses) you see a 2-1 ratio of using ideas compared to praising (remember she thinks she praises too much). Interesting is that after students responded, eight times she asked another question, went into lecture ten times, and gave directions eight times.

Row 9. She praised student initiation once and used ideas nineteen times. She asked another question fourteen times, gave directions eight times, and criticized once. After praise (row 2), students she called on continued to answer ten times. Row 3 shows she asked another question thirty-one times (okay) and gave directions thirteen times. You know this teacher well. She has a large, fragile ego. Looking at FIAS plus video data, you decide to allow her much input in the conference. You will play the leading role and let the data talk. You begin by reviewing foci intent, then gently work with columns 8 and 9, supported by videotape.

Since you've learned that a maximum of eight minutes of videotaping is sufficient and efficient, and you tape only in relation to her foci, you have two objective pieces (FIAS and video) to work with—starting with columns 8 and 9. Chances are she is not aware of the type of interaction she has with students who initiate. You bring that to her attention.

Note: You know she criticized more than FIAS matrix indicates. Since underwhelming is better than overwhelming with most teachers (especially fragile egos), you coded some of the sevens as sixes on purpose. When she sees the matrix and sees that she did criticize a bit and gave directions a lot, she'll know that she needs to improve both. You don't have to emphasize it.

There is a technique in clinical supervision that is important but hard to master. It is nonverbal and powerful. You know she criticized a lot, and she knows you know. Neither of you verbalize it, but your eyes may communicate it. She appreciates and values what you did and did not do. She will work on the criticism.

Your plan is to discuss the eights and nines and also the sixes and sevens (lightly). That's enough, and you hope her reaction will be positive.

Conference: You did what you intended, allowing her input, and letting data speak to the foci she indicated. You both work out a plan to improve the praise, reduce directions, and somewhat even out the eights and nines. Your next clinical observation will be in early April.

Clinical # 2 in April. In the pre-pre-observation, you've decided on observation date, and she'll bring the lesson plan to the pre-observation. In the pre-observation, you review the October plan and both of you decide to concentrate on the same items as before.

This observation resulted in FIAS matrix A2 (see figure 4.14).

Analysis/strategy: Column one has sixteen entries (maybe combine with praise?). You will use it in the conference, since ten were in response to student initiation, an earlier weak point. Columns 2 and 3 are closer now. Column 6 is less than last time, and column 7 has only one (*real*) entry. Stu-

	1	2	3	4	5	6	7	8	9	10	Total
1		4		3	1			2		7	
2		8	10	12		1		4	3	20	
3	4	14	6	21	7	1			7	6	
4		1						53	26	8	
5				5	7			1	1	4	
6								8		2	
7										1	
8		16	31	12	1	1		6	1	9	
9	10	7	18	11					5	9	
10	2	8	1	25	3	7	1	3	15	1	
Total	16	58	66	89	19	10	1	77	58	67	461
Column Percent											

ID = 229/30 = 7.6

Teacher Talk Columns 1-7	Student Talk Columns 8-9
56	27
% of total talk	% of total talk

Figure 4.14.   Matrix A2

dent response and initiation are much closer now. Column 10 is higher—no worry. Teacher talk and student talk did not vary much from last time. Her ID is much higher than last time.

Sequential analysis: Row 4 shows that questioning is clean—fifty-three answers from students she called on and twenty-six student initiation, a 2-1 ratio. Recall the last ratio was almost 3-1. The twos and threes in row 8 still have a 2-1 ratio= no change. Row 9 has a positive change. Including most of accepting feeling with praise we have almost = praise and use of idea when students initiate. Rows 2 and 3 are much improved. Here we see more patterns of 4-8/9-3-2, 4-8/9-3-3, and 4-8/9-2-2.

Conference: You decided to let her open the conference and state some of the positive improvements. You added that she had better balance between eights and nines and cleaner questioning technique. In your observation next October, you and she decided to concentrate on the same foci.

So she improved in many areas. You'll probably never know how much your slighting of the sevens and coding some as sixes in the first matrix made her willing to change. Maybe your eye communication this time indicated a thank you from her. It is still nonverbal and very powerful.

Now comes the important part. She improved from first observation to the second. What will you do to help her sustain that improvement? Further, she is only one of the many teachers you supervise with FIAS/clinical supervision. What will you do to help them sustain growth? Will you visit classrooms on a daily basis? Will you encourage teachers as best you can?

Case Study 2: This teacher has taught first grade at Phillips Elementary for thirteen years. This year she has been depressed. You conduct clinical supervision twice each year for each teacher.

Pre-pre-observation: You ask the teacher when she would like you to observe and remind her to bring the lesson plan to the pre-observation conference.

Pre-observation: You enter her room and say, "how are you, Clara?" She says she is somewhat depressed since her mother died last month and finds it more difficult to concentrate. Further, she is single and has no social life. You empathize as much as possible and keep the conversation going until you feel she is ready to look at her lesson plan. It appears a bit sketchy. She wants to encourage more student initiation.

Observation: She has already told the class you are coming in. You use FIAS and video to observe her.

Analysis/Strategy: As you analyze remember her condition. Her B1 matrix (see figure 4.15) shows thirty-eight praise, fifty-five use of idea (not quite a

	1	2	3	4	5	6	7	8	9	10	Total
1									1	1	
2		5	8	5	3	2		4	4	9	
3		9	12	8	18	2		3	5	2	
4				1				30	12	4	
5			2	14	52	12		2	12	6	
6			1	5	6	4	1	4	4	13	
7						1					
8		12	16	8	3	6		3	1	1	
9	1	8	13	4	8	5			1	5	
10	1	4	3	8	8	6		5	7	5	
Total	2	38	55	53	109	38	1	51	47	46	440
Column Percent											

ID = 148/149 = 1

Teacher Talk Columns	Student Talk Columns
1-7	8-9
61 ¾	21
% of total talk	% of total talk

Figure 4.15.   Matrix B1: First Frade

2-1 ratio), fifty-three questions, 109 lecture, thirty-eight giving directions, one criticism (you used the same nonverbal strategy as the secondary principal did), evenness in eight and nine, and forty-six in silence/confusion. Teacher talk is 62 percent, student talk is 21 percent, and her ID is 1.

Sequential analysis shows clean questioning—thirty answers in student response and 12 in initiation. The 8 and 9 rows show that praise and using student ideas seem okay. Perhaps the lecture and giving directions after students answer is an indication of her being depressed. The 2 and 3 rows seem okay. Given her situation, you decide to discuss lecture and giving directions. You will nurture rapport and offer guidance and see where that leads.

Conference: Clara seemed more relaxed as she looked at her video and the FIAS matrix. She agreed to lessen both lecture and giving directions. You mentioned nothing about criticism and she asked if you would semi-observe before the next clinical supervision session in April. You agreed.

Clinical #2 in April: In the pre-pre-observation, Clara reaffirmed her intention to make her lessons more student-oriented via more student initiation. You both agreed on the observation date.

Pre-observation: You made short visits to Clara's class in the intervening months and noticed that she seemed more relaxed than she did in October. She seemed ready for this observation.

Observation: This time you mentioned to the class that you will observe today. The students were used to your being in the class. No problem.

This observation resulted in FIAS matrix B2 (see figure 4.16).

Analysis/strategy: Column analysis shows a wider gap in columns 2 (38) and 3 (82) than in matrix B1. Questioning increased (66). Then the matrix showed an almost unbelievable turnabout from before. Lecture decreased from 109 to thirty-two, directions decreased from thirty-eight to seven. No criticism. Most amazing were student response decrease from fifty-one to twenty-five, and student initiation increase from forty-seven to eighty-eight.

	1	2	3	4	5	6	7	8	9	10	Total
1		3		2							
2		6	7	12				1	6	12	
3		12	9	30	11	1		1	6	6	
4			1					8	58		
5				8	12	1		2	5	4	
6								5		2	
7											
8		4	8	1	1	3		4	2	3	
9	4	12	52	6	2			2	5	5	
10	1	1	5	7	6	2		2	6	1	
Total	5	38	82	66	32	7		25	88	33	376
Column Percent											

ID = 191/39 = 4.9

Teacher Talk Columns 1-7	Student Talk Columns 8-9
61	30
% of total talk	% of total talk

Figure 4.16. Matrix B2: First Grade

Her ID was 4.9. You've never seen a change like this before. How will you handle the conference?

Conference: You began by showing Clara the matrix comparison, congratulating her, then asking how she did it. She replied that she made up her mind to achieve her objective of making the class more student centered via student initiation. Then she said she could never have done it without your understanding and help. You thanked her, and left the conference wishing that all the clinical supervision cycles were more like this one.

Summary

FIAS was developed by Ned Flanders in the 1950s and 1960s. Then, and for several years afterward, it was the most researched and widely used objective analysis system.

FIAS is a ten-item, teacher and student talk, time-coded instrument. Numbers identifying specific teacher talk and student talk categories are listed every three seconds in column form (usually twenty items/minute) on an 8-1/2 x 11 blank sheet of paper. After coding the teacher/student interaction in class, the principal pairs the numbers and tallies the pairs into a 100-square matrix. Both column analysis and the very powerful sequential analysis (from pairs) are then used to help teachers improve via the clinical supervision conference.

In addition to including some history of objective instrumentation and FIAS in particular, this chapter section provides a highly detailed, user-friendly explanation of the FIAS process. The explanation results from more than four decades of author use of the instrument in clinical supervision, as well as interaction with the clinical supervision founders.

Principals can learn the FIAS system from information and examples included in this section and then teach it to the school's teachers. As mentioned, microteaching is an excellent starter teaching method. Using it as an objective instrument to which others can be added is integral to clinical supervision. Several examples of FIAS use in the clinical cycle were also given in this section, again with a great deal of user-friendly specifics.

FAQs

If FIAS is so great in your estimation, why don't principals use it in our school? Thirty-nine years ago, Fred Wilhelms, former ASCD executive director and NASSP consultant, said, "I have a hunch that administrators and teachers have hung back from using this and other analytical systems largely because they think it is a terribly complex and difficult process. Such fears are unjustified . . . In reality, the acquisition of the necessary skills need not be viewed as any great hurdle . . . over time it will be fun." I've used FIAS for forty-four years and I'll second Wilhelms' analysis. It's great, and yes, it is fun—for both teacher and supervisor (principal).

What are some of the weaknesses of FIAS? FIAS measures only (at least it is supposed to) verbal interaction. It can tell you how many students answered questions, but not who those students are. When we pair it with several other objective instruments, it can. It also can't give you nonverbal interaction (at least it is not supposed to). Pair it with videotape on a teacher's specific objective.

What is FIAS's greatest strength or value? It, as well as clinical supervision, is used for growth of each participant, not evaluation

C. BEHAVIOR-BASED OBSERVATION

Behavior-Based Observation (BBO) instruments are used mainly in government and safety programs within agencies. BBO is another time-coded objective tool to use in clinical supervision because it can be individualized for a teacher's needs. Use it stand-alone or with FIAS for gathering objective data on student behavior. Here's how: In the preobservation

- Jointly select about four student behaviors that relate to/affect the teacher's focus. Key them a, b, c, d.
- Jointly determine the time code (three to five minutes) you will use.
- Prepare a seating chart with students' names within respective squares. Number each time period in the squares.
- When you observe, take a class behavior "picture" by marking the key for each student every x minutes. This is not as difficult as it seems. When you mark, do so only for those students not paying attention, and not for students paying attention. In most cases you'll have few keys to mark.

A completed BBO form is shown in figure 4.17. Usually you'll want to record at least ten "pictures" to reveal each student's behavior at the specific time frames. The data will afford the teacher an objective description of classroom behavior, and where problems are occurring.

Figure 4.18 shows a summary of the observations, with totals and percent of student behavior. It provides the teacher with summaries of student attentiveness or nonattentiveness.

Front of Classroom

Student 1		Student 2		Student 3		Student 4	
1 ___	6 ___	1 ___	6 ___	1 ___	6 ___	1 ___	6 ___
2 ___	7 ___	2 ___	7 ___	2 ___	7 ___	2 ___	7 ___
3 ___	8 ___	3 ___	8 ___	3 ___	8 ___	3 ___	8 ___
4 ___	9 ___	4 ___	9 ___	4 ___	9 ___	4 ___	9 ___
5 ___	10 ___	5 ___	10 ___	5 ___	10 ___	5 ___	10 ___

Student 5		Student 6		Student 7		Student 8	
1 ___	6 ___	1 ___	6 ___	1 ___	6 ___	1 ___	6 ___
2 ___	7 ___	2 ___	7 ___	2 ___	7 ___	2 ___	7 ___
3 ___	8 ___	3 ___	8 ___	3 ___	8 ___	3 ___	8 ___
4 ___	9 ___	4 ___	9 ___	4 ___	9 ___	4 ___	9 ___
5 ___	10 ___	5 ___	10 ___	5 ___	10 ___	5 ___	10 ___

Student 9		Student 10		Student 11		Student 12	
1 ___	6 ___	1 ___	6 ___	1 ___	6 ___	1 ___	6 ___
2 ___	7 ___	2 ___	7 ___	2 ___	7 ___	2 ___	7 ___
3 ___	8 ___	3 ___	8 ___	3 ___	8 ___	3 ___	8 ___
4 ___	9 ___	4 ___	9 ___	4 ___	9 ___	4 ___	9 ___
5 ___	10 ___	5 ___	10 ___	5 ___	10 ___	5 ___	10 ___

Student 13		Student 14		Student 15		Student 16	
1 ___	6 ___	1 ___	6 ___	1 ___	6 ___	1 ___	6 ___
2 ___	7 ___	2 ___	7 ___	2 ___	7 ___	2 ___	7 ___
3 ___	8 ___	3 ___	8 ___	3 ___	8 ___	3 ___	8 ___
4 ___	9 ___	4 ___	9 ___	4 ___	9 ___	4 ___	9 ___
5 ___	10 ___	5 ___	10 ___	5 ___	10 ___	5 ___	10 ___

ACTIVITY CODE

A = Paying Attention
B = Other Productive Work
C = Talking to Others
D = Non-Productive Work

TIME-FRAME CODE

1 =	6 =
2 =	7 =
3 =	8 =
4 =	9 =
5 =	10 =

Figure 4.17. Behavior Based Observation

Behavior Based Observation: Sixth Grade Math

Front of Classroom

Student 1		Student 2		Student 3		Student 4	
1 A	6 A	1 A	6 A	1 A	6 D	1 A	6 A
2 A	7 A	2 A	7 A	2 A	7 D	2 A	7 A
3 A	8 A	3 A	8 A	3 A	8 D	3 A	8 A
4 A	9 A	4 A	9 A	4 A	9 A	4 A	9 A
5 A	10 A	5 A	10 A	5 D	10 A	5 A	10 A

Student 5		Student 6		Student 7		Student 8	
1 A	6 A	1 A	6 A	1 A	6 A	1 A	6 A
2 A	7 A	2 A	7 A	2 A	7 A	2 A	7 A
3 A	8 A	3 A	8 A	3 A	8 A	3 A	8 A
4 C	9 A	4 A	9 A	4 A	9 A	4 A	9 A
5 C	10 A	5 A	10 A	5 A	10 A	5 A	10 A

Student 9		Student 10		Student 11		Student 12	
1 C	6 C	1 C	6 A	1 A	6 A	1 A	6 A
2 C	7 A	2 C	7 A	2 A	7 A	2 A	7 A
3 C	8 D	3 C	8 A	3 A	8 A	3 A	8 A
4 C	9 A	4 A	9 A	4 A	9 A	4 A	9 A
5 A	10 D	5 A	10 A	5 A	10 A	5 A	10 A

Student 13		Student 14		Student 15		Student 16	
1 A	6 A	1 A	6 A	1 A	6 A	1 A	6 A
2 A	7 A	2 A	7 A	2 A	7 A	2 A	7 A
3 A	8 A	3 A	8 A	3 A	8 A	3 A	8 A
4 A	9 A	4 A	9 A	4 A	9 A	4 A	9 A
5 A	10 A	5 A	10 A	5 A	10 A	5 A	10 A

ACTIVITY CODE
A = Paying Attention
B = Other Productive Work
C = Talking to Others
D = Non-Productive Work

TIME-FRAME CODE	
1 = 10:30 AM	6 = 10:40 AM
2 = 10:32 AM	7 = 10:42 AM
3 = 10:34 AM	8 = 10:44 AM
4 = 10:36 AM	9 = 10:46 AM
5 = 10:38 AM	10 = 10:48 AM

Figure 4.17. (*continued*)

ACTIVITY	TIME-FRAME										SUMMARY	
	1	2	3	4	5	6	7	8	9	10	Total	Percent
A. Paying Attention												
B. Other Productive Work												
C. Talking to Others												
D. Non-Productive Work												

ACTIVITY	TIME-FRAME										SUMMARY	
	1	2	3	4	5	6	7	8	9	10	Total	Percent
A. Paying Attention	14	14	16	14	14	14	15	14	16	15	146	91%
B. Other Productive Work	0	0	0	0	0	0	0	0	0	0	0	0%
C. Talking to Others	2	2	0	2	1	1	0	0	0	0	8	5%
D. Non-Productive Work	0	0	0	0	1	1	1	2	0	1	6	4%

Figure 4.18

Case Study: The following figure illustrates how two instruments can be used together for analysis. You have had several visits and a clinical supervision session with Mary, a sixth-grade teacher. She has taught there for five years without incident. This year, however, she has discipline problems. She told you that marriage problems have started. Mary is very active. She just earned a master's degree, is the teachers' union head, volunteers with local organizations, and is an avid gardener. Her husband is a laborer.

On the left side is the first column of FIAS. The first entry is 9 9, meaning that a student initiated, and the student is #9. A few numbers below is 9 15, student #15 initiated.

The set of numbers in the center of the page, as 1 --- 3, shows the student and how many times the student interacted with Mary, Thus student #1 had three interactions with her. Total # of interactions = 88.

On the right is the seating pattern you suggested in a clinical conference. Students' seats are angled toward the center of the room, Mary's desk is closer to the students, and the center is cleared for her to walk through for proximity. Right-side students, mostly minority, are by the windows (Mary's choice, not yours). The parking lot is just outside the windows. Students on the left side are next to the corridor wall. Easily apparent is her interaction pattern. Students on the left receive more attention. Students 4, 5, 7, and 8 had forty-five of the total eighty-eight interactions—*more than half for only four of twenty students.*

You observed this math class. You saw, but Mary didn't, student #5 throw the rubber chicken and hit student #1 in the head. When students started to

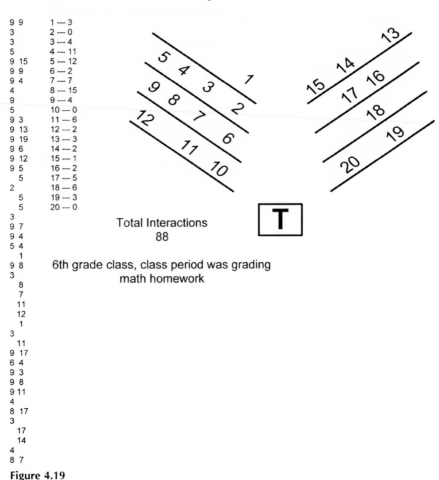

9 9	1 --- 3
3	2 --- 0
3	3 --- 4
5	4 --- 11
9 15	5 --- 12
9 9	6 --- 2
9 4	7 --- 7
4	8 --- 15
9	9 --- 4
5	10 --- 0
9 3	11 --- 6
9 13	12 --- 2
9 19	13 --- 3
9 6	14 --- 2
9 12	15 --- 1
9 5	16 --- 2
5	17 --- 5
2	18 --- 6
5	19 --- 3
5	20 --- 0
3	
9 7	
9 4	
5 4	
1	
9 8	
3	
8	
7	
11	
12	
1	
3	
11	
9 17	
6 4	
9 3	
9 8	
9 11	
4	
8 17	
3	
17	
14	
4	
8 7	

Total Interactions
88

6th grade class, class period was grading
math homework

Figure 4.19

laugh, Mary finally saw the rubber chicken and wanted to blame student #1 for disturbing the class. More laughter. Too bad you did not have a video camera to capture that data.

Interestingly, Mary did not interact with the two students closest to her, students #10 and 20. There are not any other apparent patterns, except for students #4, 5, 7, 8. You leave the room with some questions. Obviously Mary is distracted. She has no children, is feeling pretty important with her various roles, and with her newly earned educational status (master's degree), pressure is beginning to mount because of her husband's status.

You just completed the data sheet shown here. You will conference with Mary tomorrow. What will you do or say? You know she is a good teacher, but you also know she is not doing well this year, and that is beginning to affect other teachers. Students are starting to act out in their classes. Will you consult with a colleague principal? Might you suggest that Mary seek help? Can you or would you do that? Will you tell her, or does she already know that this is affecting other teachers? Will you mention the seating pattern (window side of the room) to Mary? How will you address the fact of few students receiving most of the attention/interaction?

SUMMARY

Behavior-Based Observation is a good tool to obtain an overall picture of the class through the whole period. Choosing the categories of behavior allows you opportunity to determine which student(s) may be causing a discipline problem. There are times—as when one student threw the rubber chicken and hit another student in the head—that the teacher can use to determine where the distraction originated. It is best used with video—if you can be skillful enough to do both at the same time. It takes practice.

FAQS

Is BBO practical? Yes. As I explained, it gives a good picture of the class. You can or should sit at the back of the room. That way, you will get a truer picture, since students can't look directly at you while you are calculating the instrument.

How often should you do BBO? I wouldn't suggest doing it that often. From the first observation you can obtain good information. I might also suggest that the teacher consider seating changes after viewing several of these. To do that, however, the teacher will need to change the seating pattern for the entire class.

How do you determine the categories for BBO? You and the teacher decide, according to the teacher's need or focus.

Do you need to be physically present to do a BBO? That's the best way. You might be able to do it with video, but that necessitates taping the whole period, and you later taking the time to complete the instrument.

D. TEACHER QUESTION INDEX (TQI) AND TEACHER QUESTION INDEX+ (TQI+)

Good teaching demands good questioning skills. Asking the right questions the right way at the right time may be the most important teacher activity. A colleague once mentioned that the problem with asking questions is that you may get answers—then what? All teachers strive for effective interaction in their class. Getting a student mentally involved increases the teacher's effectiveness, the students' motivation, and thus student achievement.

TQI is a tally index of questions the teacher asks. Its contents may vary for grade level, subject, student level, or individual teacher needs. It can be a stand-alone or used with FIAS.

As a stand-alone, you and the teacher cooperatively determine in pre-observation the TQI question categories you will use for the observation. Bloom's 1956 original taxonomy of educational objectives in the cognitive domain—knowledge, comprehension, application, analysis, synthesis, and evaluation—remain popular. There are many updates of Bloom's taxonomy, as well as other sources. Choose the most appropriate and useful for you.

TQI is easy to use. List the question categories on a sheet as depicted in figure 4.20. Tally each time the teacher asks a question. The index tells you how many times the teacher asked each type of question. But that's all it does.

If you want more analysis you can code students as a, b, c, d, etc. When you tally in 1 (knowledge) and teacher asked student c, just mark c. When you tally in 3 and student f answers, you mark f, and so on. That's TQI+ = which type of questions were asked, and to whom. Refer back to Mary's situation. If you used this in her class, you would have a clearer picture of the interaction.

Take TQI+ to another level with FIAS. FIAS tells you how many questions the teacher asked, *but not which student answered.* TQI+ tells you what type of question was asked to which student. Combine these. Using FIAS, code 4 (teacher asks question), and beside it code the TQI+ information (category/ type of question and student who answered). Thus, instead of just coding a 4 for FIAS, you code 43b = teacher asked a question (4), question was application (3 via Bloom), and student b answered.

You can be even more creative. Looking at the completed FIAS and TQI+ coding (the actual column numbers), you can determine what the teacher reaction to the answer was—whether the teacher praised, used student idea, asked another question, and so on.

Refer back to Mary's situation. To certain students, #s 4, 5, 7, and 8, she asked tougher questions and gave better praise. Aha! You have factual data to help her realize her actions.

Remember Jerry? He probably knew answers too but he was never called upon.

Right now you may be thinking, I'm overwhelmed—I can't do all that. *YES, YOU CAN. IT IS EASIER THAN YOU THINK. Further, when you teach*

Teacher _____ Date _____

Class/Subject _____ Time _____ to _____

Types of questions asked (tally):

Factual

Comprehension

Application

Analysis

Synthesis

Notes:

Figure 4.20.　Teacher Quation Index

teachers how to interpret and use the data for growth, both you and the teachers will have a more productive clinical experience. It does take practice, but it becomes easier and you and the teachers will like it.

The most important thing to remember is that when you use the FIAS/ TQI+, you are also able to follow the lesson too, something you can't do with more complicated objective data instruments. Hint—try it in microteaching first.

Let's take a look at coding TQI using Bloom's original categories.

1. *Knowledge = recalling facts—who, what, when, where, why.* Who invented.....? What occurred after....? When was the.........invented? Where did Martin Luther King......?

Why did ....?

2. *Comprehension = understanding, describing, comparing.* Lin, can you explain the importance of............?
3. *Application = demonstrating, implementing.* Who can think of one way to practice this principle at home this weekend?
4. *Analysis = identifying causes, inferring.* Now that we have completed the first portion, what might we expect next?
5. *Synthesis = investigating, creating.* Who could develop a method for.....?
6. *Evaluation = defending validity of, judging quality of, assessing.* How do you feel about.....?

SUMMARY

TQI is a relatively simple instrument to learn and use: Using categories you and the teacher cooperatively chose, tally each question the teacher asks during a lesson. TQI+ strengthens the instrument by including the student who answered. If you use TQI+ with FIAS, the data becomes even more valuable. When using FIAS and code question = 4, add the category of question and the student (example 43d). Then by looking at each instance afterward, you can determine the teacher response to respective students. This provides powerful analysis data. Specifically, it reveals whether teacher emphasizes critical thinking or rote.

FAQS

I like what you did with TQI+. Will it be that easy to use? Yes, once you get used to it, you'll like it.
How many categories of questions should I use? Use those that will best fit what your intent is, but I suggest not more than 4 or 5.
Can I write notes on it as well? Sure.
Should I show the notes to the teacher too? As the situation dictates.

i. Video

Videotaping equipment continues to become more sophisticated, smaller, and practical.

Gone are the adventurous days when one needed a cumbersome large tripod for a fairly large camera, a heavy reel-to-reel video recorder, various cords, a large monitor to more easily follow teacher movements and use for lesson playback during the conference, and a wired microphone to record a lesson. The first video equipment:

* required several trips to get it into the classroom
* was cumbersome (via time and class space) to set up and use for taping a lesson
* restricted time of day you could tape a lesson
* restricted where you could be in the room, thus
* hampered your using another factual data gathering instrument at the same time
* distracted students
* was light sensitive
* had reliability issues
* required operator headphones to assure you were getting a good sound level
* had limited microphone cord, and thus
* limited teacher movement, unless teacher held the microphone and moved to student who answered a question, thus delaying and interrupting the teaching process, and
* limited teacher strategy when cord would get tangled in chairs
* was cumbersome to dismantle and/or move
* limited the number of teachers you could visit each day
* restricted conference time frame. If you taped a morning lesson, you had to move the equipment quickly from the class to meet the allotted between-class time, and set the equipment up again after school either that day or another scheduled day (at the agreed-upon place for the conference).

Adventurous it was, and worrisome too, as some of the above bulleted items served for many stories. One of the more humorous stories was a colleague recalling he set up the equipment in a class at a North Carolina school, placed the microphone wire along suspended fluorescent lights, and then let the microphone physically hang down to just above the teacher's head. Of course it restricted the teacher's moves, but she was focusing on her questioning.

When he used the tape in the conference, the teacher saw herself clearly on the large monitor, but the sound was news and a weather forecast from a Nebraska radio station. Why? The wire/light combination acted as an aerial! The conference, and thus the clinical cycle, was for naught.

From that initial equipment, we advanced to beta cartridges and microphones placed into the camera. Betas were replaced by VHS, followed by smaller cartridges in the camera. All were limited in time usage. When longer-playing tapes were used, sometimes quality of picture and sound was compromised. Today's cordless cameras fit in your palm, use no tape, allow you freedom of movement in the class, and cord easily into any television for playback. What a welcome difference.

If you are in classrooms frequently, you will not have problems using videotape, even if it means you are following the teacher around the room. Why? Students and teacher are used to your being there and will act in their usual manner, ignoring you and attending to the lesson.

How best to use video?

- Discuss and agree in pre-observation.
- Tape a maximum of eight minutes. That's more than enough time.
- Tape only the elements of the agreed-upon focus. That's easy, because by instinct you will know what the teacher will do before the teacher does it. By the way, so do the students.
- Use the tape as a secondary data-gathering instrument to reinforce what your primary instrument data shows. That gives many instances of the focus behavior.
- In conference, you can play the tape, pause it, reverse, and play again if needed—depending on variables in the conference

You can use video as a stand-alone or as a complement to another objective instrument.

If you tripod, you can use FIAS, BBO, or TQI. If you hand-hold, you can devise a method to use a complementary instrument.

SUMMARY

Videotaping is much easier to use today than when it was first introduced. That should be no surprise. Video is factual and vivid. As noted above, it is best used as a secondary instrument rather than a primary one. In conference, it is quite flexible, as you can pause, replay, and so on to meet the teacher's needs.

FAQS

If I try to use video and another instrument too, is that okay? Yes. It may limit your motion around the room, but you can develop a procedure that works best for you and the teacher.

What do I do with the video after I have used it in the conference? If you can, somehow eventually get this teacher's video burned onto a disc.

Are you sure I would be able to tape only what relates to the focus? Yes, as I mentioned earlier you will get to the stage of knowing what the teacher will do next, so just turn on the recorder at that time.

E. COMBINATIONS

We have already discussed some of the combinations, so I'll try to elaborate a bit, and make it as simple as I can.

Begin with FIAS. It gives you much information. If you also needed to know how many students participated, then combine FIAS with TQI or TQI+. Or if the teacher has a specific focus that will make video a good combination for FIAS, try that. But you have to practice, because using the camera and also using FIAS requires both hands and a steady place for you to code.

Try BBO with video. Every X minutes you can code the behavior on the chart as well as capture it on video. In the conference you will have two factual objective elements that you can discuss with the teacher.

Microteaching and video are a perfect combination. Since the lesson is only five to ten minutes, you can record all of it. It is the quickest because you need to analyze fairly quickly. You can also use FIAS with microteaching. TQI is a good fit with microteaching too.

FAQS

Is it possible to just use part of FIAS rather than coding all ten numbers? Yes, thanks for asking that. Recall the diagram with just the questions (4), student answer (8 or 9), and teacher response to the answer (2, 3, 4, 5, etc). Just using 4 8, 9, 2, and 3 gives a good picture. You won't need the matrix either. You could just use the columns and circle the combinations you or the teacher wish to see. Example—teacher wants to know how much he praised. Every time you have coded 4-8-2, circle it. Or if the teacher wants to know if he used student ideas, circle the 4-8-3 entries. I like using the partial—especially when it may be an unscheduled visit or a visit the teacher asked me to make as a result of the conference.

References

Aleman, M. (1992). Redefining "Teacher," *Educational Leadership*, 50(3).

Allen, D. *Micro-teaching: A Description.* Stanford University.

ASCD information (1974). Washington, D.C.: Association for Supervision and Curriculum Development.

Brophy, J. E., & Good, T. L. (2007). *Looking in Classrooms* (10th Ed.). Boston, MA: Allyn & Bacon.

Brubacher, J. (1947). *A History of the Problems of Education.* New York: McGraw-Hill, Inc.

Bruner, J. (1974). *Toward a Theory of Instruction.* Cambridge, MA: Belknap Press.

Bynner, W. (1944). *The Way of Life According to Lao Tzu.* New York: The John Day Company

Chadsey, C., and others (1923). *The Status of the Superintendency, 1st yearbook.* Department of Superintendence. Washington, D.C.: NEA.

Cogan, M. (1973). *Clinical Supervision.* Boston: Houghton Mifflin Company.

Cooper, J. M. (2010). Classroom Teaching Skills (9th Ed.). Belmont, CA: Wadsworth Publishing.

Cornelius-White, J. H. D., & Harbaugh, A. P. (2009). *Learner-Centered Instruction: Building Relationships for Student Success.* Thousand Oaks, CA: Sage Publications.

Cornett, C. E. (1983). *What You Should Know About Teaching and Learning Styles.* Bloomington, IN: Phi Delta Kappa Educational Foundation.

Costa, A. L. (2001). *Developing Minds: A Resource Book for Teaching Thinking* (3rd Ed.). Alexandria, VA: Association for Supervision and Curriculum Development.

Coyne, M. D., Kame'enui, E. J., & Carnine, D. W. (2011). *Effective Teaching Strategies That Accommodate Diverse Learners* (4th Ed.). Upper Saddle River, NJ: Prentice Hall.

Cubberly, E. (1929). *Public School Administration.* New York: Houghton Mifflin Company

DSDI (1931). *The Fourth Yearbook of the Department of Supervisors and Directors of Instruction of the National Education Association. In Evaluation of Supervision.* New York: Teachers College Press.

Davies, D. (1953). *New Ways to Better Administration. Educational Trend.* Washington, D.C.: Arthur C. Croft Publications

Elliot, A. J. (2006). "The Hierarchical Model of Approach Avoidance Motivation." *Motivation and Emotion*, 30, 111–16.

Eye, G. G., Netzer, L., Krey, R. D. (1971). *Supervision of Instruction: A Phase of Administration* (2nd Ed.). New York: Harper & Row.

Flanders, N. (1962). "Using Interaction in the Inservice Training of Teachers," *Journal of Experimental Education.*

Flanders, N. (1962). *Helping Teachers Change Their Behavior.* United States Office of Education, Project 1721012. Ann Arbor: The University of Michigan.

Flanders, N. (1965). *Teacher Influence, Pupil Attitudes, and Achievement.* United States Department of Health, Education, and Welfare, Office of Education, Cooperative Research Monograph No. 12. Washington, D.C.: Government Printing Office.

Flanders, N. (1970). *Analyzing Teacher Behavior.* Reading, MA: Addison-Wesley Publishing Company, Inc.

Flanders, N., & Amidon, E. (1979). *A Case Study of an Educational Innovation: The History of Flanders Interaction Analysis System.* Oakland, CA: Ned Flanders.

Frymier, J. (1976). "Supervision and the Motivational Dilemma" *Journal of Research and Development in Education*, 9(2), 36–46.

Funst, N. *Interaction Analysis in Teacher Education: A Review of Studies.* ATE Research Bulletin 10. Washington, D.C.: Association of Teacher Educators.

Gagne, M., & Deci, E. (2005). "Self-Determination Theory and Work Motivation." *Journal of Organisational Behaviour*, 26, 331–62. *Journal of Sport Behaviour*, 30, 307–29.

Gagne, R. M., Wager, W. W., Golas, K. C., Keller, J. M., & Russell, J. D. (2004). *Principles of Instructional Design* (5th Ed.). Belmont, CA: Wadsworth Publishing.

Goldhammer, R. (1969). *Clinical Supervision: Special Methods for the Supervision of Teachers.* New York: Holt, Rinehart, and Winston, Inc.

Goldhammer, R., Anderson, R., & Krajewski, R. (1993). *Clinical Supervision: Special Methods for the Supervision of Teachers* (3rd Ed.). Fort Worth, TX: Harcourt Brace Jovanovich.

Good, C. V. (1959). *Dictionary of Education* (2nd Ed.). New York: McGraw-Hill.

Gross, N., & Herriott, R. (1965). *Staff Leadership in Public Schools: A Sociological Inquiry.* New York, NY: John Wiley & Sons, Inc.

Houts, P., Koerner, T., & Krajewski, R. (1979). *View from the Bridge: A Discussion. Theory Into Practice.* College of Education, The Ohio State University.

Jensen, E. P. (2008). *Brain-Based Learning: The New Paradigm of Teaching* (2nd Ed.). Thousand Oaks, CA: Corwin Press.

Journal of Research and Development in Education, theme Clinical Supervision (1976) 9(2), Athens, GA.

Joyce, B. R., & Weil, M. (2008). *Models of Teaching.* Boston, MA: Allyn & Bacon.

Keefe, J. W. (1982). *Assessing Student Learning Styles: An Overview*. Student Learning Styles and Brain Behavior-Programs, Instrumentation, Research. Reston, VA: NASSP.

Kizlik, R. J. (2010). *Tips on Becoming a Teacher*. Retrieved on February 18, 2011 from http://www.adprima.com/tipson.htm.

Krajewski, R. J. (1982). "Clinical Supervision: A Conceptual Framework." *Journal of Research and Development in Education*, 15(2), 38–43.

Krajewski, B., & Jones, B. (1997). "Student Teaching Supervision: A Cross-Cultural Dialogue." *Action in Teacher Education* 18(4), 77–82.

Likert, R. (1967). *The Human Organization*. New York: McGraw-Hill.

Maehr, M. L., Karabenick, S., & Urdan, T. (2008). *Advances in Motivation and Achievement*, Volume 15: Social Psychological Perspectives on Motivation. Bingley, Wales: Emerald.

Marzano, R. J. (1992). *A Different Kind of Classroom: Teaching With Dimensions of Learning*. Alexandria, VA: Association for Supervision and Curriculum Development.

Marzano, R. J., (2006). *The Art and Science of Teaching: A Comprehensive Framework for Effective Instruction*. Alexandria, VA: Association for Supervision and Curriculum Development.

Marzano, R. J., Brandt, R., Hughes, C., Jones, B., Presseisen, B., Rankin, S., and Suhor, C. (1988). *Dimensions of Thinking: A Framework for Curriculum and Instruction*. Alexandria, VA: Association for Supervision and Curriculum Development.

Maslow, A. H. (1954). Motivation and Personality. New York: Harper-Row.

McCarthy, B. (1990). "Using the 4MAT System to Bring Learning Styles to Schools." *Educational Leadership*, 48(2), 31–37.

McGregor, D. (2007). *Developing Thinking; Developing Learning*. Philadelphia: Open University Press.

Moallem, M. (2007). "Accommodating Individual Differences in the Design of Online Learning Environments: A Comparative Study." *Journal of Research on Technology in Education*, 40(2), 219–47.

Molnar, A., & Zahorik, J. A. (1976). *Curriculum Theory: Proceedings & Selected Papers from the Milwaukee Curriculum Theory Conference*. Alexandria, VA: Association for Supervision and Curriculum Development.

Moskowitz, G. (1967). "The Effects of Training in Interaction Analysis on the Behavior of Secondary School Teachers." *High School Journal* Oct., 17–25.

Moore, K. D. (2009). *Effective Instructional Strategies: From Theory to Practice*. Thousand Oaks, CA: Sage Publications.

Ober, R. "Predicting Student Teacher Verbal Behavior." An unpublished doctoral dissertation, The Ohio State University, Columbus Ohio, 1966.

Ober, R. (1967). "The Nature of Interaction Analysis." *High School Journal*, October, 7–16.

Palmer, G., Peters, R., & Streetman, R. (2003). "Cooperative Learning." In M. Orey (Ed.), "Emerging Perspectives on Learning, Teaching, and Technology." Retrieved February 18, 2011 from http://projects.coe.uga.edu/epltt/.

Philpott, J. (2009). *Captivating Your Class: Effective Teaching Skills*. New York: Continuum.

Pierce, P. (1935). *The Design and Development of the Public School Principalship*. Chicago: University of Chicago Press.

Rogers, C. R. (1994). *Freedom to Learn* (3rd Ed.). Upper Saddle River, NJ: Prentice Hall.

Rogers, V., and others (1952). *The American School Superintendency 30th Yearbook*, American Association of School Administrators. Washington, D.C.: NEA.

Stiggins, R. J. (2008). *Student-Involved Assessment for Learning* (5th Ed.). Upper Saddle River, NJ: Pearson Education, Inc.

Stoddard, H., and others (1933). *Educational Leadership. 11th Yearbook, Department of Superintendence*. Washington, D.C.: NEA.

Wilhelms, F. T. (1973). *Supervision in a New Key*. Washington, D.C.: Association for Supervision and Curriculum Development.

Index